Natural and Conceptual Design

# American University Studies

Series IV
English Language and Literature

Vol. 9

PETER LANG
New York · Berne · Frankfort on the Main · Nancy

Joseph M. Ditta

# Natural and Conceptual Design

## Radical Confusion in Critical Theory

**PETER LANG**
New York · Berne · Frankfort on the Main · Nancy

Library of Congress Cataloging in Publication Data

**Ditta, Joseph M., 1943–**
  Natural and conceptual design.

  (American University Studies.   Series IV, English
Language and Literature; vol. 9)
  1. Criticism.   I. Title.   II. Series.
PN81.D52   1984     801'.95      84-47541
ISBN 0-8204-0119-6


CIP-Kurztitelaufnahme der Deutschen Bibliothek

**Ditta, Joseph M.:**
Natural and conceptual design: rad. confusion
in crit. theory / Joseph M. Ditta. – New York;
Berne; Frankfort on the Main; Nancy: Lang,
1984.
  (American University Studies: Ser. 4, English
  Language and Literature; Vol. 9)
  ISBN 0-8204-0119-6

NE: American University Studies / 04

Printed by Lang Druck, Inc., Liebefeld/Berne (Switzerland)

To my wife
JoAnn
I dedicate this book

## ACKNOWLEDGMENTS

The discussion of Emily Dickinson in Part II has appeared in print in <u>Dickinson Studies</u> (June 1982).  I would like to acknowledge the generosity of Dakota Wesleyan University for its support through the Bush Foundation grants for individual scholars, and my thanks to Laura Ulvestad for her clerical assistance.

Table of Contents

# INTRODUCTION

Contemporary criticism often seems to desire the extremes, to want to stretch our credulity beyond its limits. The more unhappy we as readers of this criticism become the happier its writers become. As Montaigne observed in his infinitely less complex scholarly era, "There are more books on books than on any other subject." In our highly competitive age, it is no wonder that writers of criticism seek the extremes, for it is usually in this way that one gets noticed. But in our search for publication we have created conditions that threaten to destroy the usefulness of criticism. Since the time of Saintsbury criticism has undergone so many revolutions that its indentity as an adjunct to literature has become irretrievably lost. The critic today is less a man of literature than he was, and more a philosopher than his training gives him any right to be. Unfortunately, systematic thought and the arduous training necessary for systematic thinking would leave the critic little time to learn his literature. But philosophers are what the critics have become and strange philosophies indeed they advocate.

Thus the direction of critical thought I hope to foster stems from my belief that only a reawakening of the critic's sense of obligation to literature can rescue his work from the arcane and esoteric regions into which his desire has pushed it. What seems to me most grievous about our contemporary situation is the fact that familiarity with literature, indeed, lifelong intimacy with it, is of little use as an aid in comprehending recent critical debate. Take this as a measure or gauge, if you will, of the dimensions of the problem.

Or take, as another gauge, one of the many books which typify contemporary criticism: <u>After</u> <u>The</u> <u>New</u> <u>Criticism</u>, by Frank Lentricchia.[1] It is not my purpose here to criticize this work, though I shall be discussing it at some length later on. The book is 384 pages in length including notes. <u>Not</u> <u>a</u> <u>single</u> <u>work</u> <u>of</u> <u>literature</u> <u>is</u> <u>discussed</u> <u>in</u> <u>it</u>. An excellent gauge of the extent to which we have drifted from our home ground as critics is its index: Althusser, Bacon, Barrett, Bell, Bergson, Buber, Chomsky, Croce, Darwin, Derrida, Descartes, Dewey, Freud, Greimas, Hegel, Heidegger, Husserl, William James, Jung, Kant, Kierkegaard, Lacan, Levi-Strauss, Locke, Marcusse, Marx, Nietzsche, Pearce, Pierce, Pepper, Ricoeur, Santayanna, Sartre, Schopenhauer, Symons, Saussure, Vaihinger, Wasserman, and so on. These names are all familiar to us through criticism (though not one of them is a critic). Does this not seem an expropriation? The point is that this book is not atypical. One need only follow the discipline for a while to feel how rapidly increasing is this drift. One then begins to comprehend the reason for the vituperative, malicious attacks against such a traditional and outstanding work as M. H. Abrams' <u>Natural</u> <u>Supernaturalism</u>.[2]

In response to those who would accuse me of desiring a critical pablum, an easily digestable and safe dish of literary commentary, I would point out that a critic like Kenneth Burke, whose life has been devoted to daring speculation (and who in one place or another anticipates almost every major critical position fashionable today), had always begun with and ended in specific literary texts--"As a way in, let us begin with . . ." --and adduced his evidence not from the pronouncements and fashionable sources of the critical <u>avant-guarde</u> but from the scenes and acts, stories, stanzas and lines of the literary artist. One was "safe" with Burke, if the word must be used, because one shared with him an interest in literature.

I think it would be quite correct (and commonplace) to say that a consuming interest in literature among critics has given way to a consuming need to be interesting. One senses that there could be nothing so boring to our critics today than discussion of a literary work. It is just demode. One encounters this attitude quite undisguised in many places: Books, articles, coffee room conversation, even in the classroom.

Among the more prominent critics today, J. Hillis Miller offers us a criticism "that will, like poetry, cure the reader"; Roland Barthes offers us "an escape from boring repetition into novelty and creativity"; Stanley Fish offers "to interest us rather than bore us with soundness"; Jacques Derrida seeks a "freeplay," "amounting to a 'methodical craziness,' to produce a 'dissemination' of texts that, endless and treacherous and terrifying, liberates us to an errance joyeuse."[3]

That criticism should be interesting in its own right, that it should regard its efforts as creative and equal to the literature it was originally conceived to serve, that criticism should seek "liberation" from the confines of a subject matter and pursue curative political, social, moral, and philosophical ends are perhaps signs that a new intellectual discipline has arisen. However, it is a discipline that has little resemblance to critical activity as we formerly knew it. To be able to demonstrate lines of development from Arnold to the New Humanists of the early Twentieth Century to Eliot and Richards and the New Critics of their generation to the French dominated structuralists and post-structuralists of our contemporary period is not of itself sufficient to establish a coherence that would embrace the whole into a single discipline.

Irving Babbitt revolutionized the approach to literary criticism. After him, criticism was no longer viewed as opinion or as expressions of taste, but as an articulation of values central to moral and intellectual well-being. His influence consisted primarily in the opposition he aroused. To oppose him, critics found themselves making distinctions and considering problems that they might not otherwise have discovered. But Babbitt had a mind shaped by literature and there is hardly a conclusion drawn anywhere in his works that is not supported by, dependent on, and explained in relation to literary works. Babbitt's humanism may be considered an extra-literary force operant in and controlling his literary judgments. Nevertheless, this humanism, however limiting it may have been on his capacity to appreciate and find value in literary works, was itself a phenomenon of literary expression, and Babbitt never tired of delineating its features and debasements in the literary culture of Europe and America.

By contrast, so much is made today of methodology and its supporting terms--the whole structuralist and deconstructionist vocabulary, for example--that it is hardly possible anymore to escape the use of these terms and the concepts they animate. The real thrust of these concepts, as deconstructionist commentators never tire of stressing, is their focusing of attention on language as a system and the "decentering" of all utterance--that is, the dismissal of the subject who utters and the consequent "world of referentiality" toward which, in his innocence, the subject supposes his utterance to be directed. What remains is, of course, only the differences between the signifiers that enable them to achieve their individuality as distinct units in the system of signifiers that comprise language. By deconstructive analysis the ideas to which the signifiers point can themselves be systematized, or at least, internal contradictions discovered. By analogy, then, we can extend this system to embrace the human personality and reduce all varieties of human character to difference as it appears in the textuality of their presentation. What constitutes a human character can thus be managed as its differences from the textuality of other characters. This method of analysis enables us to eschew the ethical and social judgments by which a Babbitt discovered the values in human terms that revealed character.

The definition of a Hamlet, then, need no longer require an ethical analysis, for example, but can be achieved by a careful delineation of his differences from the texts of Polonius and Claudius, Laertes and Horatio, etc. To suppose that Hamlet has an identity that can be grasped by ethical, social, or psychological characteristics is to suppose the existence of objective referents to the vocabularies of these discourses. This is, of course, an impermissable assumption in contemporary critical theory. He has no identity but what can be found in difference. As Lacan observes: "Everything that might be considered the stuff of psychology . . . will follow the path of the signifier."[4] The consequence of this logical extension of the Saussurian linguistics is clearly the subversion of our capacity to think in traditional ways about literature. What contemporary critics who follow this school believe they are accomplishing by these post-structuralist assumptions is an escape from the dead hand of the past, an escape from such "indefensible" concepts as the self, the author, and the text. This "escape" is what constitutes the danger for criticism today and is the condition that threatens to destroy its usefulness as a branch of literary study, for it is indeed an "escape to nowhere." Without the concepts of self, author, and text, the very word "literature" ceases to have meaning. I do not believe we have yet discovered a sufficient ground for this suicide.

These tendencies are due in part to the economy and to the administration of universities which create the desperate need of faculty to publish in order to achieve tenure in an academic institution and then to retain one's reputation in order to retain salary increases. There is more to putting the problem in these skeptical terms than at first meets the eye. When the commanding figures of the day arrogate to themselves the power to decide the fate of a text, there is more at work than interest in literature.

> How often have we heard gory talk about "the
> battle of the new criticism," about "total
> war," about firing broadsides" designed "to
> blast the other side into oblivion," about
> "counterattacks," "missiles," and "barrages."
> The notion seems to be spreading that each
> author must kill his predecessors, or that,
> as Tzvetan Todorov has put it, if the text
> is to survive, the descriptive commentary
> must die; if the commentary lives, it will
> have killed the text.[5]

To this I will add only the observation that there is nothing more sublimely indifferent to the commanding figures of today than yesterday's texts. Todorov is, of course, speaking about the poetic text and its critical commentary, and this leads to a further observation, namely, that there has grown inexorably since the Anglo-American New Critical movement a notion, more a passionate belief, that the critical text exists in hot competition with the creative literature that it now shares a shelf with in our university book stores. However, I do not want to insist on this argument. For the time being, it is only necessary that I point out the difference between a critical commentary and a poem, and on this difference it is part of my intention in this work to insist: the critical commentary is a way of reading, the poem is what is read. This simple distinction has seemingly been lost in the dense forest of jargon and over-subtle linguistic-philosophical-analytic brush of our contemporary scene. And yet, on this difference everything depends.

Critical theory, if it is ever to rise above interminable controversy, must at some point in its self-elaboration be concerned with the problems of internal consistency. Psychoanalysis, structuralism and post-structuralism, and Marxism, the subjects of the three chapters of part one of the present work, are major critical modes primarily because of their claims to scientific, methodological, and philosophical validity. I concentrate in these chapters, therefore, on what I regard to be crucial conceptual and theoretical failures in each. Then, in part two, I offer not so much an alternative approach to these major schools but a theoretical justification for the return of critical theory and practice to a consideration of the literariness of works of literature. This return would also be a much needed corrective to the responsibility prevalent among those writers who take an almost narcissistic interest in their own theorizing. In the introduction to his recent book, Is There A Text In This Class?, Stanley Fish, for example, explains: "What interests me about many of the essays collected here is the fact that I could not write them today. I could not write them today because both the form of their arguments and the form of the problems those arguments address are a function of assumptions I no longer hold."[6] This fascination with one's own thought processes in the critical act has a decidedly negative impact on one's relation to the literature: critical procedure becomes an end-in-itself, and the question of adequacy of the procedure to the texts upon which it works is lost amid one's fascination with one's own theses about them. How else explain the collecting and publishing of essays one had written in the past and which no longer reflect one's thinking? The implication, of course, is that tomorrow a new book of old views must be published. The critical theory which once gave us the poem as poem is now giving us criticism as criticism.

What falls away, and what has fallen away, inevitably, is the humanistic assumption which regards the work of literature as an imitation of experience--in the service of implying a view of life--with a formal and artistic coherence, and the notion that there is ultimately a correspondence between this artistic coherence and philosophical coherence; that is, the organization of mental processes which occur outside literature.[7] The three schools of criticism I discuss in part one all fail, for various reasons specific to each, to regard the literary work and the effort of reading as an ideal grounded in "a purely personal cultivation." They fail essentially because this basic humanistic comprehension of the nature of literary art has given way to a spurious scientism of methodology. Criticism is a <u>value</u> oriented enterprise and is so because the relationship between consciousness and reality is epitomized in the relationship between literature and truth. The multiple correspondences in this formula are the matters which critics must come to grips with in order to do justice to literary art. The notion of Conceptual Design I discuss in part two is an attempt to discover, from the specifically modern kinds of failures dominating criticism today, new ground for a reconsideration of these views.

NOTES

[1]Frank Lentricchia, After The New Criticism (Chicago: University of Chicago Press, 1980). I list authors quoted in the text at such length here not to tire the reader but because the cumulative effect of this list lends force to my argument. Croce, Bell, Santayanna, and in part Bergson were aestheticians, and their work is indeed relevant to literary criticism--but it is seldom that their specifically aesthetic insights are cited.

[2]For an extended discussion of the content of these vituperative attacks, especially in the commentaries of Jerome J. McGann, "Romanticism and the Embarrassments of Critical Tradition," and J. Hillis Miller, "Tradition and Difference," see Wayne C. Booth's chapter on M. H. Abrams in Critical Understanding: The Powers and Limits of Pluralism (Chicago: University of Chicago Press, 1979), pp. 139-94.

[3]See Wayne C. Booth's characterization of contemporary criticism from which I have quoted here in Critical Understanding, pp. 197ff.

[4]See Malcolm Bowie, "Jacques Lacan," in Structuralism and Since: From Levi-Strauss to Derrida (New York: Oxford University Press, 1979), p. 132.

[5]Booth, p. 220.

[6]Stanley Fish, <u>Is There A Text In This Class?</u> (Cambridge, Massachusetts:  Harvard University Press, 1980), p. 1.

[7]See Rene Wellek and Austin Warren, <u>Theory of Literature</u> (New York:  Harcourt, Brace & World, Inc. 1956), pp. 34-36.

NATURAL AND CONCEPTUAL DESIGN:
A RADICAL CONFUSION IN CRITICAL THEORY

PART I

CHAPTER 1

PSYCHOANALYSIS AND LITERARY CRITICISM:
THEORETICAL AND PRACTICAL DIFFICULTIES

The essential point to notice is that psychoanalysis seems to show that the artist is
initially by tendency a neurotic, but that
in becoming an artist he as it were escapes
the ultimate fate of his tendency and through
art finds his way back to reality. I think it
will be seen now where psycho-analysis can be
of some assistance to the critic--namely, in
the verification of the reality of the sublimation of any given neurotic tendency.
                    (Herbert Read, "Psycho-Analysis
                          and Criticism")


Pope was a hunchback and a dwarf; Byron had a club
foot; Proust was an asthmatic neurotic of partly
Jewish descent; Keats was shorter than other men;
Thomas Wolfe, much taller . . . . Dubious, certainly,
is the widespread view that neuroticism--and
'compensation'--differentiate artists from . . . .
other 'contemplatives' . . . .
                    (Rene Wellek, Theory of Literature)


     In his essay, "Anaesthetic Criticism," Frederick Crews
observed that the "simple fact that literature is made and
enjoyed by human minds guarantees its accessibility to study in
terms of broad principles of psychic and social functioning."[1]
He argues that the point seems too obvious to dwell on but for
the resistance with which it is met among the very group "to
whom it should be most axiomatic, professional students of
literature." Elsewhere, Crews claims that by using

psychoanalytic assumptions, "a critic can show how a writer's public intention was evidently deflected by a private obsession." Freudian reasoning, he notes, whatever its shortcomings, is a useful critical enterprise.[2]

This enterprise, however, must cope with two important criticisms. The first, a common one, which has generally been granted by psychoanalytic critics, is that the psychoanalytic approach to literary studies shifts the focus of critical judgment from the work to non-literary determinants of the work. The second, more important criticism, however, suggests that this shift is in its very nature problematical, so much so that the value of all attempts at psychoanalytic criticism are shaded by doubt. Once I have delineated this problem and demonstrated its essentially epistemological character, I will examine the practice of one of our most prominent critics of the school and show how and why the "axiomatic" basis of his practice leads him into confusion and irrelevance at best, and at worst into a fatal misunderstanding of the nature of literary meaning.

Let us begin by taking up the question of meaning, for this question lies at the heart of all critical difficulties, and ask what, in the psychoanalytic method, the critic anticipates as meaning. Superficially, the psychoanalytic critic tries to "make sense" of the literary text, but his concern is governed by principles of psychic functioning which, in their very nature, require him to attend to the anomalous details in the work. "Being at bottom a theory of how conflicting demands are adjusted and merged," Frederick Crews contends, "psychoanalysis is quite prepared for literature's mixed intentions, dissociations of effect from ideational content, hints of atonement for uncommitted acts, bursts of vindictiveness and sentimentality, and ironies that seem to occupy some middle ground between satire and self-criticism."[3] Because such phenomena are frequently neglected by "professional students of literature," the argument goes, the psychoanalytic critic is able to make fuller sense of his literary texts "than could the most impressive instances of a rival criticism."[4]

The traditional reply to this position is the obvious one, namely, that the psychoanalytic critic is in fact analyzing, via the verbal tactics of the author as they are set in the permanency of the finished poem or fiction, not the work of art but the inherently private psychic constitution of its author. This retort, besides being obvious and an extreme simplification, is nevertheless cogent ˙and it raises the crucial issue with regard to literary studies. I might phrase the issue in these terms: if the adjective "literary" means anything, does its meaning function in a restrictive sense, limiting and qualifying the kinds of things we can apply it to and the meanings we may therefore anticipate in them, or are we free to construe the word in its broadest and most general sense as meaning anything written or spoken? My purpose is to apply the issue as I have stated it to the problem of the psychoanalytic approach to literature. This problem can be phrased, I think, in the following terms: however circumscribed or limited "the range of evidence" from which the psychoanalytic critic works, that is, however faithful he is to the matter in his text, what is the status of his conclusions? Are they conclusions about literature, psychology, pathology, or metapsychology? Are they conclusions about the meanings the author repressed or displaced? About human psychic functioning? About the analytic method itself?

Recall that Freud's discussions of DaVinci and Michaelangelo, for example, were intended not as critical analyses of their works but as applications of psychoanalytic theory to cultural phenomena in the interest of demonstrating and validating psychoanalytic principles as applied to the larger sphere of civilization. However we decide upon the status of the conclusions reached on the basis of psychoanalytic principles, we must next ask the question as to whether the critic can validly apply his principles to something as indifferent, passive and unresponsive to him as a literary text. The question of validity is crucial, for it is the essence of the Freudian method to <u>begin</u> analysis with dream-texts or other symbolic manifestations, and through the patient's own accounting of such inner experiences to derive the insights that are peculiarly psychoanalytic in nature. Thus, these two critical questions will govern my discussion; together, they constitute the problematic that must be resolved in order for psychoanalytic theory to be fruitfully applied to literature. In my opinion, they are not resolvable insofar as literary studies are concerned, though as a problematic they are not relevant to the therapist-patient situation, where psychoanalytic theory was forged and where it properly belongs.

I

There are two related characteristics of psychoanalysis which together comprise a formidable argument for and justification of the application of psychoanalytic principles to the interpretation of literary texts. The first of these is the fact that the analytic situation takes place in language. The patient's symptoms, delusions, dreams, illusions, etc., are revealed in therapy sessions through the act of speech. These phenomena, what Paul Ricoeur calls the semantics of desire, are regarded as symbolic manifestations or displaced representations of psychic maladjustment. Similarly, this symbolic behavior is itself regarded as language, with its own semantics and syntax. "Analytic experience unfolds in the field of speech" observes Ricoeur, and "within this field, what comes to light is another language, dissociated from common language, and which presents itself to be deciphered through its meaningful effects--symptoms, dreams, various formations, etc."[5] Because the psychoanalyst is concerned with interpreting the meaning for the patient of his story as it unfolds, his interpretive methodology is of utmost importance.

It is the provision of the methodology, the hermeneutics of psychoanalysis, that marks the greatest contribution of Freud to the study of the human mind. This leads us to the second characteristic of psychoanalysis that would seem especially to qualify the application of its principles to the interpretation of literary texts.

Because the libidinal energy of the psychism is channeled by the unique displacements, distortions, sublimations, repressions and impulsions through which it runs its course in the life history of the patient, the psychoanalyst must be highly skilled at interpreting the signs of this behavior and its meanings for the patient. The study of these libidinal drives is called energetics, and it is specifically in relation to the expression of the effects of energetics in the patient's psychical history that a hermeneutics is necessary. One of the objects of Paul Ricoeur's important book on Freud is to demonstrate the interrelationships between hermeneutics and energetics in analytic theory. It is on the basis of this interrelationship that Ricoeur insists on classifying psychoanalysis as an interpretive science rather than a natural science, in which causative discourse predominates. "It is correct to say that 'all behavior is part of a historical series'; it is correct to speak in this way in order to render analytic language homogeneous with the language of the genetic sciences. However, it must not be forgotten that in analysis, the real history is merely a clue to the figurative history through which the patient arrives at self-understanding; for the analyst, the important thing is this figurative history."[6]

Given these two characteristics of psychoanalysis, i.e. that it takes place in language and that it requires an interpretive methodology to grasp the figurative content of the special language of desire through which the psychism expresses itself, it is hard to reject the claim of the psychoanalytic critic that he has a great deal to offer in the way of interpretation to the professional study of literature. Problems arise, however, when we discover that the context of language in which the analyst works is a context different in kind from that which we experience in literature, and the hermeneutic that guides the analyst to this interpretation of the "figurative history" of his patient cannot be applied to a literary text.

Let us take up the last of these two points as our first objective. In The Interpretation of Dreams, Freud offers the following caution on the interpretation of dream symbolism:

> I should like to utter an express warning
> against overestimating the importance of
> symbols in dream-interpretation, against
> restricting the work of translating dreams
> merely to translating symbols and against
> abandoning the technique of making use of
> the dreamer's associations. The two tech-
> niques of dream-interpretation must be
> complementary to each other, but both in
> practice and in theory the first place
> continues to be held by the procedure . . . .
> which attributes a decisive significance to
> the comments made by the dreamer.[7]

Freud is careful to point out here that dream symbolism is only a part of the total context that the analyst must interpret, and itself not even a decisive part. What is decisive, in the analytic process, is the patient's own reactions to and understanding of the symbolism in his or her dreams. Of course, the patient is seldom aware that this or that particular image in a dream is symbolic. The analyst's main function in the procedure is to point out to the patient the possible symbolic significance of dream content. Freud demonstrates this procedure in his discussion of one patient's dream in which a hat figures as an image of male genitals.  "It is quite remarkable how the dreamer behaved after this interpretation.  She withdrew her description of the hat, and would not admit that she had said the two side pieces were hanging down . . . .  She was quiet for a while, and then found the courage to ask why it was that one of her husband's testicles was lower than the other, and whether it was the same with all men."[8]  Freud goes on to remark that from other cases he might assume that the hat could also stand for the female genitals.  What is important for us in this example is that it demonstrates how the analyst's interpretation is dependent on the patient's responses to his  guesses.   But  before  the analyst is prepared to offer his interpretation of certain dream symbols, he must first have acquired some knowledge of the patient's psychic history.

Contrasting the methods of the behavioral psychologist with those of the psychoanalyst, Paul Ricoeur observes:

> The psychologist speaks of environmental variables.  How are they operative within analytic theory?  For the analyst, these are not facts as known by an outside observer. What is important to the analyst are the dimensions of the environment as "believed" by the subject; what is pertinent to him is not the fact, but the meaning the fact has assumed in the subject's history . . . . The object of the analyst's study is the meaning for the subject of the same events the psychologist regards as an observer . . . . For the analyst, therefore, behavior is not a dependent variable observable from without, but is rather the expressions of the changes of meaning of the subject's history, as they are revealed in the analytical situation.[9]

These observations set in relief the problem I have been trying to define in regard to the application of analytic theory to literary structures. The issue is both theoretical and practical (though my primary concern in this part of the discussion is with the theoretical aspects). The epistemological framework in which the literary critic works and from which he derives his methodology is constituted by two things: 1. the literary tradition (both creative work and critical response); 2. the work at hand (whether it is the collective work of an author or a single representative of it). I omit from this framework language itself and the vast area of cultural reference language makes possible because the literary critic and the psychoanalyst have these in common and, consequently, this part of the framework does not serve to set them apart or to distinguish their methodologies. The critic, however, of whatever persuasion, comes to his work as an outside observer. All the signs, signals, expressive signs, symbols that he deals with are variables from the point of view of the tradition within which they exist and of which they form a part, and are equally variables from the point of view of the individual work, though in a different way than in the former. In the latter sense, they are variables because as the critic's estimation of them undergoes revision they are reconstituted into different meanings. But always, these contents of the literary work are impassive and remain indifferent to the operations the critic performs on them. In the context of his epistemological framework, one may characterize the critic's procedure as an interweaving process of observation and interpretation (bearing in mind that by "interpretation" we do not mean "explanation" in the causative sense of the natural sciences). By contrast, the epistemological framework in which the psychoanalyst works is constituted by Freudian theory and the analytical situation, which includes the verbal behavior, silences, postures, attitudes, and expressive movements of the patient; and we may

characterize the analyst's procedures as an interweaving
process of <u>interaction</u> <u>and</u> <u>interpretation</u>.[10]

The difference between these characterizations leads to a
further observation, namely, that while the psychoanalyst's
results are meaningful in terms of <u>motivation</u> (the patient's),
the critic's results are meaningful in terms of <u>contemplation</u>,
unless we posit art as a means to action and thus reduce it to
its propagandistic function solely. This difference suggests
that, unlike the analyst in the analytical situation, the
psychoanalytic critic is making the fundamental error of
seeking, in the linguistic anomalies of his text, causative
antecedents. By contrast, the analyst is concerned with the
meaning for the patient of his interpretation. Thus his
guesses are essentially <u>heuristic</u> in their function. The
psychoanalytic critic, however, would regard this difference as
inconsequential and charge that so stating it actually begs the
question with respect to the purposes of criticism generally.
This is not a tangential issue, but very much at the center of
the argument. Because of the analytic nature of his
perceptions and judgments, the psychoanalytic critic must
regard the text as something "<u>to see through</u> and best explained
by something other than--even contradicting--itself."[11] But I
do not think the issue as I have stated it begs the question at
all, but rather sets in relief even further the problem I have
been trying to define. For example, in the first essay of his
book <u>Out</u> <u>of</u> <u>My</u> <u>System</u>, Frederick Crews argues:

> The psychologist offers us, with a pre-
> sumption we are likely to resent, a view of
> the writer's innermost preoccupations, a
> technique for exposing those preoccupations
> behind the defenses erected against them,
> and a dynamic explanation of how the literary
> work is received and judged. It is not merely
> that literature illustrates psychoanalytic

ideas . . . . but that the psychoanalyst alone
undertakes to find motives for every rendered
detail.[12]

I will concede that psychoanalysis perhaps alone among
literary tools can explain the dynamics of how the literary
work is received and judged. These are motivations that lie
squarely within its province and to the extent that it does
this convincingly, it is an important part of literary studies.
But it is a rash judgment to claim, on the basis of a literary
text which the analyst can observe (as all critics do) but not
interact with, that he can find the motives for every rendered
detail. Freud himself was aware of this problem and took care
to distinguish the seeming dreamlike structures of literary
artists from the dreams produced in sleep. "Most of the
artificial dreams contrived by the poets are intended for some
such symbolic interpretation, for they reproduce the thought
conceived by the poet in a guise not unlike the disguise which
we are wont to find in our dreams."[13] The terms "artificial,"
"contrived," "reproduce," and "guise" as opposed to "disguise,"
all suggest the problem of the degree of conscious purpose
Freud understood to be involved in literary production, and
without the analytic situation in the context of which alone
the analyst can disentangle the artistic from the defensive and
adaptive motives, the analytic approach must remain essentially
problematic. Unless all guesses of motives are made within the
design of the literary structure and their meanings with
respect to that structure are limited to what the structure
expresses as a literary artifact, the psychoanalyst has no more
authority than anyone else to interpret it.

There is a very real sense in which we can claim an
equivalence (on an epistemological level) between the literary
text and the dream. Indeed it is often the case that dreams
provide the writer not only with his material, but also with
the form in which it is presented.[14] But as Paul Ricoeur
reminds us:

> It is not the dream as dreamed that can be
> interpreted, but rather the text of the dream
> account; analysis attempts to substitute for
> this text another text that could be called
> the primitive speech of desire. Thus analysis
> moves from one meaning to another meaning; it
> is not desires as such that are placed at the
> center of analysis; but rather their language.[15]

This "language" that is placed at the center of analysis is the
verbal behavior, silences, postures, expressive movements,
etc., that constitute the analytic situation. In this
context, dreams provide only a starting point. The actual
text, a text different in kind from that experienced in
literature, that is analyzed is the dream-accounting of the
patient, and as we have been pointing out, this accounting
includes linguistic as well as other behavior. There is thus a
layering of meaning, with the dream-as-dreamed forming a
foundation that is so far from being decisive as to become
obscured and lost sight of as the layers of meaning accumulate.

By contrast, the literary work retains our attention and
holds it only insofar as it succeeds in externalizing through
its own language structures what is necessary to support a
sense of meaning. In his Mimesis, Eric Auerbach demonstrates
how in the Homeric style this externalizing of phenomena serves
to delineate and situate, and thus represent, the concrete
contents of experience that form the world of Homer's
characters. The more dream-like story of Abraham and Isaac in
the Hebrew tradition, though subjectve in its mode of
expression as Auerbach shows, nevertheless depends upon an
elaborated ethical tradition external to but carried in each
word of the text. The Homeric and the Hebraic styles are
prototypes of the later Western tradition, and although they
function differently with regard to mimesis, they both depend
upon a communal experience to which they appeal and from which

their language derives its referential character.

Can the psychoanalyst transfer his method of inquiry into the psyche to his activities as a reader of literary texts? Cut off from communal experiences as the determining character of a text's referentiality and committed to the proposition that the individual adaptive and defensive strategies of the psyche determine a text's referentiality, he must seek another text layered over the original as the source of the original's meaning. Since he cannot acquire by analysis this "text of the dream account," he must provide such a text himself. There are only two sources from which he can derive this text. Either he can interrogate the author, or he must derive this text from his own mind. As we shall see later, Norman Holland in his major books, The Dynamics of Literary Response, Poems in Persons, and Five Readers Reading, frankly adopts the latter alternative.

But to return to our subject, the "language" that is placed at the center of analysis is constituted in part by the subject's account of his or her dreams and in part also by the manner of the telling. These, then, are replaced by the analyst by what Ricoeur calls "the primitive speech of desire," which was derived in analytic practice from the commonalities of behavior among many patients and which now serves as both theoretical interpretation of human psychic behavior in general and as a guide to the interpretation of a specific pshychic history. The semantics of this "primitive speech" are what constitute the hermeneutics by which the analyst finds meaning in the dynamics of repression, sublimation, cathexis, etc.[16] When we observe the practice of psychoanalytic criticism, it is obvious from the start that the critic's basic assumption, and methodology dervied from it, is that this "primitive speech of desire" can be used as a hermeneutic to "decode" the literary text. Thus, the critic must regard the formal rules of rhetoric and prosodic conventions as well as variations of these in the actual text as providing that second level of discourse, or at least part of it, that constitutes the "telling" or accounting which is so significant in the analytic situation. This leads him into a double difficulty, multiplying his problems both theorectically and practically. It is his response to this situation that causes Norman Holland to resort to a perfectly logical but finally self-destructive critical practice in which psychoanalytic criticism comes to its final resting place.

I do not refer here to the problem of reductionism, perhaps one of the most frequent accusations hurled at psychoanalytic criticism. Reductionism is the charge that the psychoanalytic critic reduces all literature to variations on a single theme. This is another problem, however, and not my concern here. Rather, the difficulty I refer to is a procedural one with theoretical implications related to the problem I have defined above. The problem of reductionism, however, is tangentially related to this difficulty, for the genius of psychoanalytic terminology drags the interpretation of literary texts down to the level of those orders of experience from which this terminolgoy is derived. I am less concerned with reductionism, however, than I am with misrepresentation.

As I have noted above, in the analytic situation, the interactive process is characteristic of the epistemological framework in which the analyst works, and the interpretations acheived by the analyst in this process function heuristically, so that as analysis proceeds, the subject becomes more enlightened about his own problems and thus more reliable as a participant in the interactive process. Roy Shafer, in his article "Narration in the Psychoanalytic Dialogue," stresses this problem of reliability in analytic interpretation.[17] "The competent psychoanalyst deals with telling as a form of showing and with showing as a form of telling. Everything in analysis is both communication and demonstration." The validity of analytic interpretation is thus enhanced by this twofold condition of communication and demonstration. "Situated in the present," Schafer continues:

> the analyst takes the telling also as a showing, noting, for example, when that content is introduced, for it might be a way of forestalling the emotional experiencing of the immediate transference relationship; noting also how that content is being told, for it might be told flatly, histrionically, in a masochistically self-pitying or grandiosely triumphant way . . . the analyst also attends to cues that the analysand, consciously or unconsciously, may be an unreliable narrator: highlighting the persecutory actions of others and minimizing the analysand's seduction of the persecutor to persecute; slanting the story in order to block out significant periods in his/her life . . . . All of which is to say that the analyst takes the telling as performance as well as content.[18]

As analysis proceeds, both the analyst and the patient undergo change, presumably in the direction of increasing validity of interpretation and enlightenment. Thus, the distinction we observed earlier between verbal behavior and the silences, postures, expressive movements, attitudes, etc., that constitute the "language" that is placed at the center of analysis must be regarded as crucial to interpretation, because these parts of the analytic situation are mutually informative. Without, as Schafer says, the "showing," the validity of the "telling" cannot be taken for granted.

We have seen, then, one aspect of the double difficulty the practice of psychoanalytic criticism is involved in. By considering the literary text as an epistemological equivalent of the dream-as-dreamed, the critic lacks the dream-account and without the dream-accounting process in which he must function as a participant, he also lacks the experiential grounds upon which his interpretation must rest for its validity. This practical difficulty leads to theoretical uncertainties that cannot, in the nature of things, be quieted. But this is only one side of the double difficulty I am attempting to explain. The other, I think, is more serious.

The psychoanalytic critic, as noted earlier, must regard the rhetorical and prosodic conventions as well as their variations as they appear in the literary text as equivalent, on an epistemological level, to the "manner" or "showing" aspect of that which is missing from his relationship to the text. To put it more clearly, when analyzing a text, the critic must regard its content as equivalent to the dream-as-dreamed, and its presentational and formal characteristics as equivalent to that aspect of the dream-accounting that reveals manner.[19] The point or goal to be achieved by this practice is not enlightenment of the author's motivational complexes and thus a condition of greater self-control and satisfaction for him, but an elucidation of his, the author's, identity for our contemplation in and through the literary text. Whether the text reveals patterns of order on the social, mythic or metaphysical levels, the psychoanalytic critic must ultimately regard meaning as a figuration of a specific human psychic history. This goal underlies the critical practice and, indeed, is the only warrantable motive for the undertaking of a psychoanalytical critical project.

But as Paul Ricoeur argues, "It is one and the same enterprise to understand Freudianism as a discourse about the subject and to discover that the subject is never the subject one thinks it is."[20] The psychoanalyst, although he interacts with and interprets the defensive and adaptive motivational dynamics of the subject, nevertheless remains an outsider in relation to the subject's self-identity. Psychoanalysis is essentially a "theory of instincts and their vicissitudes."

The source of its terminolgy and "the primitive speech of desire" that it substitutes for the subject's "telling" and "showing" is the commonalities of human psychic behavior generally. This is the basis of the charge of reductionism.

As Paul Ricoeur points out, the "I am," one's essential identity that is the focus of self-reflection, "is the very factor that escapes analytic conceptualization":

> Are we to look for it in the consciousness? Consciousness presents itself as the representative of the external world, as a surface function, as a mere sign or character in the developed formula Cs-Pcpt. Are we looking for the ego? What we find is the id. Shall we turn from the id to the dominating agency? What we meet is the superego. Shall we try to reach the ego in its function of affirmation, defense, expansion? What we discover is narcissism, the great screen between self and oneself. The circle has come full turn and the ego of the cogito sum has escaped each time.[21]

This is no cause for despair. Psychoanalysis functions by virtue of its capacity to make generic applications to individual, special circumstances. But the identity of these special circumstances--persons like you and me--remains beyond its scope. Once again, we see the program of the psychoanalytic approach to literature disappear at the moment we scrutinize it. Psychoanalysis functions therapeutically on the level of individual behavior via the application of theoretical principles that are generic in terms of the understanding they help us to. But it cannot provide a reflective portrait of a human identity for our contemplation, most especially if its only contact with that identity is the literary text.

## II

So far I have attempted to identify the discrepencies between the psychoanalytic project for literature and the basis of psychoanalysis in the analytic situation. We have seen how and why the criterion of judgment in the analytic situation cannot be applied to literary texts. We have seen that the epistemological function of language in the analytic situation has no parallel in the literary text and that the hermeneutic which guides the analyst to his interpretation of the figurative history of the analysand cannot be applied to literature. Lastly, we have suggested that the fundamental goal of psychoanalytical criticism is itself theoretically unsound.

However, all of these criticism presume that the psychoanalytic critic approaches the literary text as a meaningful structure of words that can be understood by others and that, given certain agreements among readers with regard to the kind of meaning to be discovered there and the methodology for ascertaining it, this understanding can be shared. I want to stress that this assumption is a common one and has been the basis not only of psychoanalytical criticism but of all criticism, and that in varied forms this assumption is applied to all language use. Now, to skirt the criticisms which I have been at pains to point out and to place psychoanalytic criticism on a footing that cannot be reproached by these theoretical difficulties, it is necessary to establish an alternative assumption, one that would not be subject to these attacks.

Such an assumption would be the diametric opposite of the one I have just described. The problem, however, with such an assumption is that it would fly in the face of all critical doctrine and in and of itself be so radical as to require a revision of our understanding of not only literature but of all language use. These difficulties do not deter Norman Holland, who has developed a psychoanalytical approach to literature that is, on the basis of such an assumption, unassailable. However, his practice is in its nature not subject to any criticism at all and is for this reason philosophically suspect. But more importantly, a concept of literary meaning cannot be developed from his theories and practice (this is an argument that can be applied to psychoanalytic criticism generally, but which is particularly relevant with Holland): the term "literature" must remain an empty signifier in his thought.

In his book Poems in Persons, which Holland claims represents major breakthroughs in the understanding of literature and of ourselves, Holland remarks, "The dynamics by which people experience literature reveals a highly subjective recreation, and, in a way, the real puzzle is not why people react differently to the same work, but how they could ever share the same response."[22] To explain this remark will involve us in an excursion into psychoanalytic theory along with Holland, who selects as his starting point "the single most important contribution to psychoanalysis by someone other than Freud: Robert Waelder's classic: 'The Principle of Multiple Function'" (p. 45).

According to Waelder the principle expresses the ego's tendency to select an action in response to some need that satisfies demands from several sources within the psyche and in reality. This is described as a tendency towards inertia--achieving a maximum of effect with a minimum of effort. "More exactly," Holland comments, "Waelder sees the ego as mediating among four structures or functions that act on it: id and superego, reality and the repetition compulsion."

> These four forces acting on the ego show a
> neat symmetry. The id pushes for the expression
> of sexual and aggressive drives; the superego
> tries to inhibit them. The repetition compulsion
> tends to keep the ego doing what it did before,

while reality (because it constantly changes)
constantly demands new solutions from the ego.
These four forces press on the ego, and in that
sense the ego passively mediates among them. But
the ego also assigns itself the task of testing
and probing the four forces, and in this sense
the ego actively seeks out problems and solutions.
Every psychic act results from the ego's actively
and passively seeking an optimum balance of the
forces impinging on it (pp. 45-46).

The ego's every choice of action, according to Holland,
represents a new compromise among the ego's active and passive
relations with the four forces to which it responds. Waelder's
theory forms the basis of Holland's speculations. To build
upon it, he now turns his thought to a host of studies.
Briefly, Holland notes that Freud observed how "The sexual
behavior of a human being often lays down the pattern for all
his other modes of reacting to life." Studies have shown how
"the concept of rationalization suggests how ideas that pretend
to be purely intellectual may serve instinctual or defensive
strategies." Other studies, he observes, suggest that
ideologies and value systems reflect "a mixture of conscious
and unconscious needs," that a person's moral behavior (his
superego style) "reflects his personality just as much as his
instinctual life," that prose style "matches the total
personality," and that the cognitive and perceptive style of
the ego describes its dealings with drives or anxieties as well
as its everyday functioning, etc. "In effect," argues Holland,
"all these clinicians and theorists are saying the same thing:
there is one style that operates in all the ego's activities,
in all its mediations among the four forces it must respond to"
(pp. 47-48).

Holland sums the matter up: "The mode of reconciling
various tasks to one another is characteristic for a given

personality. Thus the ego's habitual modes of adjustment to the external world, the id, and the superego, and the characteristic types of combining these modes with one another constitute character" (p. 48). Following Yeats, Holland calls this personal style of adjustment a "myth," because the term helps to establish the idea of organic unity in the psyche. This "myth" is an "identity-theme," which, once understood as a feature of the psyche, enables us to form "the concept of a primary identity as an invariant the transformations of which we could call development (p. 50). This "identity-theme" cannot change. Thus, "The perception of the 'whole person' means the process of abstracting an invariant from the multitude of tranformations" (p. 50).

Essentially, I have no quarrel with these ideas. I do quarrel, however, with the use to which Holland puts them. The creative writer, he argues, when engaged in the act of writing, is "simply" finding a solution to the demands set by inner and outer reality, and the "writing itself--even the very manner and matter--works out a personal style that pervades the multiple functioning of the ego" (p. 57). Thus, as Holland sees it, even craftsmanship "satisfies multiple needs of drive and defense." "Forms in poems act like defenses in life, and defenses, as we have seen, to become part of one's style or character, must satisfy drives as well as manage them." Again, "To be a formal craftsman one must be able to satisfy drives by his very formalism" (p. 56). It may be argued that literary studies have long recognized these observations in its understanding of voice in literary texts. But Holland's idea is essentially radical and has grave implications with regard to the reading of texts. For Holland, creative writing is the acting out of the underlying myth that is one's identity-theme, the invariant that is the common property of all one's adaptive and defensive behavior.

However, this myth is negatively intended in the acts of distortion as disguise, falsification, illusion and the forms of misunderstanding, and can only be elicited in analysis, as indeed Holland demonstrates by his selection of H. D. as the "Maker's Mind" to probe for this purpose, the analysis of which is made possible by her memoire of her sessions with Freud. Holland selects H. D. as his "Maker's Mind," infers her "identity-theme" from her record of analysis and what is known of her biography, determines her myth and demonstrates how it controlled not only her poetry, but her emotional and intellectual life as well. Presumably, a writer's personal myth cannot be extracted from the poetry alone. Since there is no analytical situation to facilitate interpretation, Holland asks, "How can we know a poet's or novelist's mind except tautologically--by the very poems and fantasies whose creation we want to explain? We can't" (p. 6). Except, of course, in the case of H. D., who left us a memoire of her analysis with Freud.

Thus, Holland effectively skirts the isse I raised above with regard to the problem of decoding a text in terms of the primitive speech of desire. Holland recognizes that texts are inadequate for this purpose. Once we recognize this, however, we are left with uninterpretable literary exercises. How do we cope with them, since obviously texts have been read for generations and people frequently believed they understood them? The first problem is to account for the writer's desire to write, and the second problem is to account for the reader's reading. The first is disposed of easily enough: "To the extent one particular activity (like writing) functions multiply for us, we become committed to it, and it takes on the status of a permanent and preferred solution. Some of those preferred solutions prove so satisfactory as to give rise to the feeling many creative writers describe of being driven, as by an inner compulsion, back to the typewriter. This, then, is the writer's demiurge, his daimon and Muse: the creative style which stabilizes the psychic economy which is his and his alone" (p. 57). The writer writes, then, because this is an effective way to compromise with and balance the deamnds of the four forces. That is, he enjoys it. But since his products are essentially uninterpretable (from the psychoanalytic view--bear in mind that Holland's solutions are meant to rescue psychoanalytic criticism, not account universally for the literary process and the act of reading), why does the reader read? Essentially, the reader reads to "re-enact his own character," or myth, in the "raw material" of the poem. In this manner, Holland reverses the basic assumption we discussed above with regard to the ontological status of the poem or fiction.

Holland's answer to the second problem--why a reader reads--requires some explanation. Because his ingenuity has been applauded for some time and because he has--more than any other critic of the school--tailored his work to meet the essential problems of psychoanalytic criticism we discussed above, I must consider his solutions in some depth. In one sense, they are eminently logical solutions, yet in another they lead to a theoretical perspective that denies the very possibility of literature.

Since, according to Holland, the literary work is a product of its maker's adaptive and defensive mechanisms (and meaningful only in the sense that the writer successfully balances the four forces which impinge on him in the act of writing), the precondition for poetic experience in the reader "is that the reader build for himslef out of the raw material of the work his particular pattern of adaptation and defense. If he cannot or will not, then he can have no positive experience of the work" (p. 96). The manner in which the reader builds his particular pattern of adaptation and defense involves a set of four principles that governs the way he "re-creates" a literary work: First, there is "one general, overarching law: style creates itself." According to Holland, the reader in the act of reading composes a literary experience in his own particular lifestyle: "line by line and episode by episode, he responds positively to those elements that, at any given point in the work, he perceives as acting out what he would characteristically expect from another being in such circumstances. What cannot be perceived as acting out his expectations he responds negatively or remains indifferent to" (pp. 77-78).

This principle that "style creates itself" is a crucial step in the ordering of Holland's thought. I cannot testify to what extent this principle is generated by experience in the analytical situation. But I suspect that an essential confusion between interpretation in the analytical situation and interpretation in literary situations lies at the heart of Holland's perception of the "overarching" nature of this principle. But I must reserve criticism for later and present now Holland's principles complete. He continues: "To respond positively, to gratify expectations this way, a reader must be able to create his characteristic modes of adaptation and defense from the words he is reading. This is the second principle, and the most exacting: defense must match defense." By this, Holland means that the reader must re-enact for himself precisely, from the raw material of the text, those structures by which he wards off anxiety in real life. "Once he has done so . . . the reader can very freely shape for himself from the literary materials he has admitted a fantasy that gives him pleasure, and this is the third principle. He projects into the work a fantasy that yields the pleasure he characteristically seeks." Perhaps recognizing that he is here allowing his reader too much liberty from the stringencies of language, Holland proposes a fourth principle: the reader must "make sense" of the text: "He transforms the fantasy he has projected into it by means of the defensive structures he has created from it to arrive at an intellectual or moral 'point' in what he has read. Thus the reader comes full circle. In reading, as in life, he transforms his fantasies into socially and personally acceptable modes of being, but in reading, as contrasted to life, he derives the materials he transforms, not from experience, but from the words and stringencies of a literary work. Style creates itself."

Holland attempts to demonstrate these four principles by analyzing two readers in order to elicit their identity-themes, and by then discussing their responses to a poem by H. D. in order to compare the projections of identity-themes among all three--H. D. and the two readers. There is a great deal to criticize here, both in terms of the theorectical basis of his study and the methodology by which it is executed. Let us begin with the four principles.

The first thing one will notice is that there is a difference in kind between the first three principles and the last. Presumably, when a reader responds to a text in terms of the first principle, and creates his characteristic modes of adaptation and defense in terms of the second, then shapes for himself a pleasing fantasy on the basis of his earlier responses, he is acting out of psychological necessity; that is, he reads this way because his psyche is so constructed as to require him to. If this determinism did not underlie the reading process, there would be no sense in calling these descriptions of the reading process principles. The fourth principle, the transforming of the projected fantasy into an intellectual or moral "point," clearly is not of the same psychological order as the others. Thus to say that in reading, as in life, one transforms one's fantasies into socially acceptable modes of being is to be very naive. What a different place the world would be were it true! "Teach us to mourn our nature," the poet laments, and Nero's fantasies could hardly compel us to believe that men transform their pleasures into socially acceptable modes of being. But clearly, readers do derive intellectual and moral "points"--notice how carefully Holland avoids the traditional term of "theme" and similarly calls interpretations of texts "responses"--from the texts they read. How do they do this, if the reading process is as it is characterized in the first three principles? In spite of Holland's description of the reading process, readers can derive moral "points" only if they will to transfrom their fantasies into socially acceptable modes of being. There is no necessity for such a transformation to take place. Since necessity in not an underlying factor, as it is in the functioning of the other three principles, we may more rightly expect readers to remain on the level of response to the text that returns greatest pleasure--sheer fantasizing in order to yield the pleasure they characteristically seek. Thus, according to Holland's first three principles, we should expect the reading process to precipitate narcissistic identity-theme pleasure excursions. But people who read frequently among a wide variety of authors would not characterize their reading experience in these terms. The argument that skilled readers are more likely to conform to Holland's fourth principle is, on the face of it, unsound. My criticism is based on deterministic psychological processes which, if truly functioning, would hold for all readers. Similarly, if Holland argues that he is describing learned experience, then he necessarily gives up his case--we can learn other ways to read, construe and interpret literary texts. I would argue, of course, that we not only can but do, and that the important thing is to understand what actually takes place and to then improve our capacities to teach and respond to literature. It is for this reason--to make his description of the reading process conform to our actual habits--that he must logically posit his fourth principle. One may legitimatly argue that in this case negating the consequent results in negating the antecedents. But we can examine the three prior principles and negate them singly on their own terms.

Holland's first principle--that style creates itself--is grounded in the assumption that one's identity-theme determines one's expectations from life and thus controls the character of one's responses to life. I earlier suggested that I suspected a confusion here of processes that take place in the analytical situation with the literary experience. The psychoanalyst may, for example, in understanding the origin of a pathological condition, suddenly perceive its influence in a wide range of behavior. Holland recognizes this when he observes that Freud "generalized from the Wolf-Man about the unity implied by a psychoanalytic explanation, 'how, after a certain phase of the treatment, everything seemed to converge upon it, and how later, in the synthesis, the most various and remarkable results radiated out from it; how not only the large problems but the smallest peculiarities in the history of the case were cleared up by this single explanation'" (p. 49). The theoretical problems attendant upon the analogy between the effect of trauma on a person's behavior and the effects of one's identity-theme on his behavior is beyond my scope. But if one translates Holland's first principle into analytical discourse, the phrase "style creates itself" becomes "personality is a consequence of psychoogical adaptations and defenses," where "personality" is a substitute for "identity-theme" on the one hand or "neurosis" on the other. We come no closer, by this formulation, to understanding the processes of literary comprehension.

The second principle--that defense must match defense-- is based on implications derived from the first. If we assume that when the reader reads he is immersed "with oceanic raptness" in his own self, it follows that we must logically consider the words of the text to be nothing more than a series of "excitations and counterexcitations . . . set in motion and directed" by the reader himslef (p. 84). That is, we must consider the words and their ordering "raw material," on an ontological level indistinguishable from the data of the senses in every unguarded moment of life, or guarded moment for that matter. Holland's insistence that the words of the text impose syntactic and semantic constraints on the reader but are nevertheless raw material in the act of reading is a genuine puzzle. Nevertheless, his second principle purports to describe the structuring process by which the reader "re-creates" the text in his own image. It is clear from the underlying assumption that the word "re-create" is only superficially relevant to the process being described. There is no "re-creation" of the text taking place in the mind of the reader--he is creating it for himself from raw material: "All (readers) will try to build an experience from some or all of the words--the raw materials--the writer left behind him . . . one ego builds its characteristic functioning out of creations which are characteristic functions of another ego" (pp. 147-48).

Insofar as the text represents a prior act of creation in the mind of the author, the reader may be thought of as re-creating it when he reads. But there is an ontological difference between the two creations, such that the text represents a primary act on each count. There is thus no "recreation" involved in the usual sense of mimesis. The text as written and the text as read have in common only the raw material of which they are comprised. In order to understand the text produced by the author one must understand his identity-theme, which cannot be construed from the text. Similarly, to understand a reader's response, one must know his identity-theme. In this way, Holland makes psychoanalytic theory and practice absolutely necessary to literary criticism. For this reason alone scepticism is in order. But it is clear from the implications of the first two principles that the term "literary" is deprived of all meaning by Holland. If the reader composes the raw material of the text in ways by which he characteristically "wards off anxiety in real life," then the act of reading is psychologically indistinguishable from non-literary behavior. Thus, Holland does not explain the literary process so much as he explains it away.

As for the third principle--projecting into the work a fantasy that yields the pleasure one characteristically seeks--aside from the solipsism it implies (together with the other two), it presumes too limited a view of the range and intensity of human experience. I would ask merely how it is possible to fantasize characteristic pleasure in:

> An aged man is but a paltry thing,
> A tattered coat upon a stick, unless
> Soul clap its hands and sing, and louder sing,
> For every tatter in its mortal dress.
> > (W. B. Yeats)

> Clear water in a brilliant bowl,
> Pink and white carnations. The light
> In the room more like snowy air,
> Reflecting snow.
> > (Wallace Stevens)

> Force should be right; or rather, right and wrong--
> Between whose endless jar justice resides--
> Should lose their names, and so should justice too.
> Then everything includes itself in power,
> Power into will, will into appetite;
> And appetite, a universal wolf,
> So doubly seconded with will and power
> Must make perforce a universal prey,
> And last eat up himself.
> > (Shakespeare)

Even a cursory examination of these passages is sufficient to indicate how unlikely it is that we, as readers, project into the lines we read our characteristic pleasures--Stevens' aesthetic sensibility could not be more at variance with Yeats' personal and Shakespeare's political-philosophical concerns. In each of these instances we hear the author's characteristic voice, and I have selected them quite at random, browsing

through pages of different books. I might have selected more
telling passages; for instance, a short objectivist poem by
Louis Zukofsky, a stanza from Sylvia Plath's "Daddy" or lines
from Whitman's "Song of Myself," and ended with a passage from
Johnson's "The Vanity of Human Wishes."

If style creates itself and we, as readers, project our
characteristic pleasures in the raw material of the poem, how
is it that we hear Yeats' voice so clearly in his lines and can
readily distinguish lines of his from lines of, say, Robert
Frost? Does each person's myth or style construct itself over
and over again with the reading of every poem? Some readers
have read thousands of poems, from all periods in the history
of our language. Are we creating in each experience our own
style over and over again? If so, how boring! But more to the
point, how is it that we can recognize a poet's voice and
determine a theme as "in character" _for_ _him_? How is it what we
can understand his vision of the world and know it as something
distinct from our own visions of it?

The most damaging criticism of Holland's work, however,
has to do with the methodology by which he carries it out.
His books, Poems in Persons and Five Readers Reading, purport
to be experimental, and his conclusions to be derived
empirically from the evidence. No scientist, however, would
accept his methodology, and in a science court he would be
readily indicted for loading his experiment. What Holland
wants to demonstrate is that the reader constructs his meaning
from the poem in terms that are determined by his or her own
adaptational and defensive adjustments to the pressures of
inner and outer reality, the same processes by which, in coping
with non-literary life experience, the individual builds and
expresses his or her identity. In order to demonstrate the
workings of the reader's re-creation of the poem "so as to
re-enact his own character," Holland offers two readers
discussing a poem by H. D., each of whom he has analyzed in
order to describe their "identity-themes." After presenting

us with his analyses, he shows how in their responses to H.
D.'s "There is a Spell," they each construct an interpretation
of it that is in fact an expression of their own
"identity-themes." Here is where the problem of method
interposes itself.

After the reading of the poem, Holland asks the following
questions (pp. 68-77): "Well, how did you respond?" The
reader conveys a brief impression. Then, "What does he (the
poet, who is not identified) seem to be saying?" Again, the
reader "responds" by offering feelings about what the poem
seems to be saying. "Are there any phrases that appeal to you
particularly?" The reader then talks about what "interested"
her. Then, "Suppose I asked you if you could just sort of run
down through the poem, picking up words or phrases that
intrigued you." And again, the reader "responds" in a
characteristically impressionistic manner and after a few
comments stops abruptly. Holland encourages, "You don't have
to do everything, just do what catches your eye." After an
interpretive comment by the reader about the bitterness implied
by a certain passage, Holland asks, "Do you like that? Does
that statement make you feel good or not so good?" And so on.
It must be stressed at this point that the poem in quesiton,
"There is a Spell," is thoroughly suited to this kind of
questioning. If you assume beforehand that your reader is
going to project, it follows that the poem chosen to work
with should be suited to that end. "There is a Spell" is a
poem about psychic defenses and adaptations, written in short
lines with rapid phrasings and a shifting, flowing imagery that
is dreamy and very indirect and symbolic. It is the kind of
poem that critics would have called "obscure in the modernist
mode" fifty years ago. The selection of this poem and the
manner of questioning pre-determine the outcome. It is not
surprising, therefore, to find the reader projecting private
fantasies, especially when she is asked to do so, encouraged to
do so by the analyst.

What Holland demonstrates is the efficacy of an analytic method to probe a person's personality and, in his zeal, he confuses literary response, which is a highly trained response to an extremely highly organized structure of words, with the diffuse, emotive, uncontrolled, impressionistic and free-associating response that the analyst has learned can reveal the psychic dispositon of a patient.[23] That poems can be used in this way is neither surprising nor new. Poetry therapy has been around for some time.[24] But the genuinely harmful effects of Holland's work are the attitudes of indulgence it encourages on the part of teachers and the unmitigated self-indulgence it encourages in readers. Self-indulgence leads to the impossibility of sharing, of achieving insight into other human minds and emotions. It also necessarily cuts one off from aesthetic appreciation. But worse, self-indulgence blinds one to the community value of art. Unless the community can play its role as the source of a work's referentiality, the value of art, especially literature, can never be more than that of a mirror of a reader's unique psychic constitution, and the human impulse to a "personal cultivation"--which manifests itself as an end in all human achievement--deprived of its meaning in this context, must eventually yield to solipism everywhere.

III

In his discussion of the epistemological controversey over the motive-cause distinction in psychoanalysis, the distinction that some psychoanalytic theorists have attempted to blend in order to compromise with behaviorism, Paul Ricoeur argues that psychoanalysis is not an observational science. The statements that psychoanalysis makes do not constitute a "causal discourse of the natural sciences." "Since it deals with psychical reality, psychoanalysis speaks not of causes but of motives."[25] The difficulty arises because though in practice the analyst appeals to motives, intentions, meanings, in theory these are treated as "psychical antecedents" to be discovered as "real causes" of real facts of behavior. These "real causes" of real facts of behavior, the argument runs, can only lead to a "gratuitous multiplication of dubious entities" which compete with the sole facts "open to observation and verification, the facts of physiology." However, Ricoeur counters by observing that "Freud's originality consists in maintaining that the strange phenomena which had previously been left to physiology are explainable in terms of intentional ideas." Insofar as the relationship between motive and language is such that it is possible to give a verbal account of motives, what distinguishes a rational agent from nonrational creatures is the extension of the area of rationality to which a patient can be brought by such verbal accounts. "The object of analytic therapy is to extend the patient's area of rationality, to replace impulsive conduct by controlled conduct."

Thus, motives must be regarded as a "region of being distinct from the region of nature and capable of being considered according to the generality or singularity of its temporal sequences." Therefore, when the behaviorist speaks of environmental variables which as a psychologist he regards as an observer, what he does not realize is that "what is important to the analyst are the dimensions of the environment as 'believed' by the subject; what is pertinent to him is not the fact, but the meaning the fact has assumed in the subject's history." The objective of the analyst's study "is the meaning for the subject of the same events the psychologist regards as an observer and sets up as environmental variables." For the analyst, therefore, Ricoeur continues, "behavior is not a dependent variable observable from without, but is rather the expression of the changes of meaning of the subject's history, as they are revealed in the analytical situation."

What this argument illustrates, and what Ricoeur's answer to it tends to confirm, is the extremely private and unique nature of the meaningful, of the symbolic, of the numinous, in psychical experience. In order to penetrate it, the analyst requires a hermeneutic method that cannot work independently of the total psyche of the patient. The analyst's hermeneutic requires, first of all, a certain responsiveness and sensitivity to the meaningful on the part of the analyst; secondly, it requires a dream-text or other symbolic experiences on which to focus; and thirdly, and most importantly, it requires the presence of the analysand, his or her added verbal accounts and total behavior in the analytical situation in order to map out a directional strategy of interpretation.

In literary criticism it is seldom possible to work from a conjunction of all three of these categories. The poetic tradition may indeed be thought of as a tradition of strategies to supply the missing elements from which interpretation may proceed. This is why biographical criticism is so often irrelevant to our understanding of an author's work. Although he does not work consciously in a psychoanalytic perspective, the biographical critic tries to supply the "added accounts" that complete the analyst's hermeneutic. He does this because it is natural to suppose that the life enters the work, and because it is in the nature of things that such interpretation of individual behavior requires the three categories of the analyst's hermeneutic. But the poem is not an instance of "individual behavior" with a private and unique history behind its meaningfulness that can only be understood by reference to the poet's life. Nor is the reader's response a product of "individual behavior," comprehensible only within the context of a knowledge of his or her psychic history. Quite the contrary, the poem does contain in itself, in the form of its conceptual design (the construction of which is a part, inevitably, of the history of poetic tradition), the writer's strategy for its comprehensibility independently of himself. Concepts are in their nature shareable mental phenomena.

Designs--of all sorts--imposed upon the conceptual content represented in a community's language are thus comprehensible not only in principle but obviously so in practice; to deny this is to deny at the same time the meaning of this very sentence, which denial would constitute a tacit admission of comprehension.

If the conceptual content of a community's language were not shareable, neither would be its emotions; lacking a conceptually organized consciousness apprehensible in terms of its perceivable intentionality, the tradition of reading could hardly have got started and could hardly have continued in a long uninterrupted history until now, when the problematics of reading have begun to raise doubts about the possibility of reading a text at all--a problematics that is perceived as such primarily because of the influence of pyschoanalytic criticism and the blending of psychoanalytics and structural linguistics as an academic discipline, as, for example, in the school that follows Jacques Lacan. In the tradition, content achieves its status as a conceptual design, as a poem, by the multifaceted nature of its meaningfulness, that is, the bringing together and dispersal outward of disparate material at the same time. The orchestration of the multiple effects of figures and tropes into a single entity--the organization of the constituents of a design into a comprehensible pattern--is of the essence of poetry. It is thus on the level of design that we recognize the poem as poem and are able to distinguish it from discourse. This is why poetry is not straight talk, and why straight talk that passes itself off as poetry is never successful, is never regarded by critics as estimable poetry.

NOTES

[1]Frederick    Crews,    "Anaesthetic    Criticism,"    in
Psychoanalysis And Literary Process, ed. Frederick Crews
(Cambridge, Massachusetts: Winthrop Publishers, 1970), p. 1.

[2]Frederick Crews, "Reductionism and its Discontents," in
Out of My System: Psychoanalysis, Ideology, and Critical
Method (New York: Oxford University Press, 1975), p. 168.
Apparently, when the Diagnostic and Statistical Manual (1980)
of the American Psychiatric Association pronounced the concept
of neurosis devoid of meaning, the psychoanalytic critic
(Crews?) no longer could depend upon theoretical support for
his claim to find meaning in the "anomalous details" of the
literary work which indicated the "private obsessions" of the
author. Neurosis hunting, at a stroke, was illegitimized. How
else account for Crews' astonishingly testy, almost ruthless
condemnation of Freudianism?   Freudian psychoanalysis, he
writes, is "so conceptually muddled and empirically dubious
that it does not warrant belief." "As everyone knows," Crews
argues,   "Freud   explained   intellectual   resistance   to
psychoanalysis in terms of injured human pride. His discovery
that our minds are enthralled by repressed wishes, he announced
without undue humility on his own part, was the third great
blow to anthropocentrism following those administered by
Copernicus and Darwin. Yet it is curious how readily many of
us absorbed the putative insult and defended it as what it
distinctly is not, a scientifically confirmed truth. The real

question to be resolved is not why people resisted a doctrine that found in every physician a deflected sadist, in every artist a former dabbler in his own feces, in every infant a murderous and incestuous schemer, in every decent act the sublimation of a barbaric impulse. The question is rather why so many people fell cheerfully into line with these and equally lurid ideas, expounded with no more proof than the say-so of a compelling stylist." See "Analysis Terminable," Commentary, July (1980), pp. 32-33 and note 19, p. 33.

Crews's recantation is almost violent and is indicative (if I may be so bold) of a profound emotional as well as intellectual change on his part. The recantation, however, does not invalidate his earlier positions quoted in this chapter, for these are the basic reasonings of the psychoanalytic approach to literature which, Crews apart, is the object of my concern here.

[3]Crews, Psychoanalysis and Literary Process, p. 15.

[4]Crews, Psychoanalysis and Literary Process, p. 5.

[5]Paul Ricoeur, Freud and Philosophy: An Essay on Interpretation (New Haven: Yale University Press, 1970), pp. 366-67.

[6]Ricoeur, p. 369.

[7]A. A. Brill, trans., The Basic Writings of Sigmund Freud (New York: The Modern Library, 1938), p. 375. Underscoring mine.

[8]Brill, p. 376.

[9]Ricoeur, p. 364. Underscoring Mine.

[10]Ricoeur, p. 364. See footnote.

[11]Crews, _Out of My System_, p. 5.

[12]Crews, _Out of My System_, pp. 4-5.

[13]Brill, p. 189. Underscoring mine.

[14]For two very good accounts of these phenomena, see Richard Wilbur, "Walking to Sleep," and John Hollander, "The Dream of the Trumpeter," in _Dreamworks: An Interdisciplinary Quarterly_, 1:2, Summer (1980).

[15]Ricoeur, pp. 5-6.

[16]This subject is discussed at length in Ricoeur, chap. 1, pp. 3-20.

[17]Roy Schafer, "Narration in the Psychoanalytic Dialogue," _Critical Inquiry_, 7:1, 1980.

[18]Schafer, pp. 38-39. Underscoring mine.

[19]For an intrinsically interesting example of this methodology, see David Leverenz, _"Moby-Dick"_, in Crews, _Psychoanalysis and Literary Process_.

[20]Ricoeur, p. 420.

[21]Ricoeur, pp. 420-421.

[22]Norman Holland, _Poems in Persons: An Introduction to the Psychoanalysis of Literature_ (New York: W. W. Norton & Co., Inc. 1975), p. 2. Because Holland represents this book as a condensation of his _5 Readers Reading_ and an introduction to his basic principles in _The Dynamics of Literary Response_, I have selected it as his most succinct statement of his

positions.  All further references to this work will appear in
the text.

[23]At one point, even Crews lost his patience with this
aspect of Holland's method:  "No Freudian has taken greater
pains to make psychoanalysis accountable for subtle differences
of genre and effect, and none has shown greater diffidence
about armchair diagnosis of authors."  Yet, Crews observes,
Holland's method, "if followed to the letter, could hardly fail
to result in reductionist criticism . . . . Although he makes
gestures of coexistence toward many styles of criticism,
Holland nevertheless declares that 'psychoanalytic meaning
underlies all the others'--a fact which can be announced in
advance of any given instance, since, in Holland's view, the
true purpose of even the most artifice-laden work is to enable
a "core fantasy" to manifest itself in a respectable disguise."
See "Reductionism and Its Discontents," in Out of My System, p.
171.

[24]See Jack J. Leedy, M.D. ed., Poetry Therapy:  The Use of
Poetry in Treatment of Emotional Disorders (Philadelphia: J. B.
Lippencott Co., 1968), and the work of Buck and Kramer,
"Creative Potential in Schizophrenia," Psychiatry, 40 (May,
1977), pp. 146-61.

[25]Ricoeur, pp. 360-64.  This and the following passages by
Ricoeur are from these pages.

CHAPTER 2

CONCEPTUAL WEAKNESSES
IN STRUCTURALIST AND POST-STRUCTURALIST THOUGHT

We read and understand ourselves as we follow the
operations of our understanding and, more important,
as we experience the limits of our understanding.
To know oneself is to study the intersubjective
processes of articulation and interpretation by
which we emerge as part of a world.  He who does
not write--he who does not actively take up and
work upon this system--is himself "written" by
the system.  He becomes the product of a culture
which eludes him.

(Jonathan Culler, Structuralist
Poetics)

One of the most rigorous structuralist principles is the
premise that the self is a construct formed by cultural systems
over which the individual has no control.  The relevance of
this "principle" to literary studies is the implication it
bears in regard to the literary text.  How must one regard the
text if one believes that its author is a construct of the
cultural systems that produced it?  Northrop Frye, in his
"Polemical Introduction" to Anatomy of Criticism, remarks that
art, "like nature, has to be distinguished from the systematic
study of it, which is criticism.  It is therefore impossible to
'learn literature':  one learns about it in a certain way, but
what one learns, transitively, is the criticism of
literature."[1]  There is a dualism in Frye's statement:  there
exists a work of art on the one hand and an organized body
of knowledge about it on the other.  This dualism is achieved
on the basis of an analogy between nature and our organized
bodies of knowledge about nature we call science:  "Physics is

an organized body of knowledge about nature, and a student of it says that he is learning physics, not nature."[2]

I believe this analogy is, ultimately, a very misleading one--for it implies an equivalence between nature and works of art that is not to my mind apparent and which may in the end be harmful. But for now, I want to point out that Frye leaves open, in this formulation of the relation between literature and criticism, the problem area of the "experience" of such works. Clearly, this "experience" is the medium between the literature (which, as Frye says, we cannot learn) and our critical ways of looking at it--experience is the bridge between the two, and I don't think Frye would have been ready to burn this bridge when he wrote the Anatomy.

But the structuralist premise that the self is a construct formed by cultural systems over which it has no control does precisely this. The text must inevitably be conceived as a trace neither produced by a writer nor experienced by a reader in the act of reading. The subject, both as author and reader, is constituted by the play of systems. The perception of structure in a poem (or in any language act) is thus an imposition of certain conventions of reading, which themselves are constitutents of the cultural systems that produced the text in the first place.[3]

The problem of the relations between the author, the reader, and the text thus give rise to the most formidable paradox in the post-structuralist criticism: the conception of a literary activity that takes place in but independently of a human environment. Speech and writing alike, in this criticism, are conceived as structured by the generative power of difference--conceived as a system that allows the units of language to achieve distinctness and thus bear meaning. But meaning itself is conceived as a product of this same generative power. It is this paradox that I wish to explore in this chapter, recognizing that no criticism of it will ultimately influence those who find the philosophy that underlies it congenial to their termperaments.

The paradox and the premise from which it derives are the especially loved children of the post-structuralist movement. But their true progenitor is Saussure's Course in General Linguistics, which is a problematic text at best, since its form as a text is not Saussure's but that of his students who took his course in general linguistics at the University of Geneva in the academic years 1906-7, 1908-9, and 1910-11.[4] The text is a reconstruction of his editors from the notes of his students together with manuscript materials and notes left by Saussure. But Saussure's most important ideas clearly rise above whatever problems might be contingent upon their presentation. Essentially, these can be listed (and our familiarity with them by this time obviates any need for lengthy introduction) as the seminal distinctions of: 1. langue and parole; 2. synchronic and diachronic; 3. the paradigmatic and syntagmatic; 4. the arbitrary nature of the lingustic sign; 5. the notion of "difference"; 6. the idea of "structure."[5]

Simply put, Saussure conceived of language as existing in a perpetual present, with its own internal coherence and consistencies. He distinguishes this language from its historical appearances in the acts of performance much as a symphony can be distinguished from its performances.[6] This distinction enabled Saussure to distinguish between the study of language externally in terms of its historical appearances by following the appearance of isolated linguistic phenomena and internally as a complete coherent whole or structure. By structure, Saussure understood essentially what Anglo-American New Critics meant by organic form, though Emile Benvineste, one of Saussure's most important interpreters, seems to regard this concept as essentially European[7]: "The arrangement of a whole in parts and the demonstrable coherence of these reciprocally conditioned parts in the whole."[8] Thus "diachrony," the appearance of language in performance, could be considered a succession of "synchronies." "The temporal model proposed by Saussure is that of a series of complete systems succeeding each other in time."[9] But the central question for Saussure was the nature of the linguistic signs that comprise the system of langue.

Saussure argued that signs are arbitrary and conventional. As such, there could be nothing in their nature that establishes their identity. Each sign is defined, then, not by any property of the sign itself, but by its differences from other signs.

> If words stood for pre-existing concepts, they would all have exact equivalents in meaning from one language to the next; but this is not true. French uses louer (une maison) "let (a house)" indifferently to mean both "pay for" and "receive payment for," whereas German uses two words, mieten and vermieten; . . . . Instead of pre-existing ideas then, we find in all the foregoing examples values emanating from the system. When they are said to correspond to concepts, it is understood that the concepts are purely differential and defined not by their positive content but negatively by their relations with the other terms of the system. Their most precise characteristic is in being what others are not.[10]

Thus the sign is conceived as a purely relational unit. It is at this point that Saussure takes the logical step which produces the critical weakness in his thought and reverberates into our time in the thought of Derrida and post-structuralist thinkers generally. This step is what gives

such figures as Barthes, Lacan, and Derrida their primary force
as originators.

Saussure concludes that since linguistic signs can be
defined only by the differences that distinguish them one from
another, then in language there is only difference, without
positive terms.

> Since one vocal image is no better suited
> than the next for what it is commissioned
> to express, it is evident, even a priori,
> that a segment of language can never in
> the final analysis be based on anything
> except its noncoincidence with the rest . . . .
> Signs function, then, not through their
> intrinsic value but through their relative
> position.[11]

This view of the linguistic sign is a drastic departure from
the nineteenth century substantialist views of correspondence
between symbol or image or organic form and processes in nature
that stand as their referents or meanings.

Saussure's relational and differential view of langue
would deny any end point, referent, or "transcendental
signified" to the sign because differences are never presences
in or among the signs, but are absences. Thus, "the
distinguishing characteristic of the sign--but the one that is
least apparent at first sight--is that in some way it always
eludes the individual or social will."[12] I say that this
notion of the sign as a relational unit the identity of which
can be conceived only in terms of difference without positive
terms is a weakness in concept because, as a definition, it
pertains to signs as viewed from only a single perspective.
When considering the nature of the sign as an observer of
langue, where one's goal is to identify the features of
language that enable it to function as a system, merely, then

the use of the concept of "difference without positive terms" becomes a tool that enables one to consider language in its "synchronous solidarity."

It is quite acceptable from both the common sense view and from an epistemological view to argue that the study of language must confine itself to "relations between mutually conditioned elements of a system." Problems arise, however, when the perspective adopted is broadened to include both language (langue) and the uses to which language is put (parole). The question to ask is why this broadening is forced, especially in the face of so much opposition and in the face of common sense. The motive behind it is complex and I will be discussing it at some length later on. But the effect of this broadening is to absorb the executive features of language into the study of its systemic features, to the point where only these systemic features are given recognition as constituting the essence of language.

"Such an idea of difference (difference without positive terms)," observes one commentator, "punctures the mystifying notion of a transcendental signified--a signified which is said to exist positively and independently of a signifier at an untouchable distance from discourse."[13] The second part of this sentence illustrates one aspect of the motive for the position taken. But it suffers from an illogic that is hard to excuse: "and which could command the relational or lateral play of signifiers at an untouchable distance from discourse." What the structuralists and post-structuralists want is an intentionality governed by the conjunction of language and performance, an intentionality that owes nothing to a problematical "objective" world, undirected by it and under no constraints imposed by "positive terms" derived from it. This rejection of the Cartesian dualism however, leads to another dualism, and one fraught with logical and moral problems (cf. the analytic/systemic opposition discussed near the end of this chapter).

However, in the interest of maintaining this position, structuralists assume that it is necessary to posit a system of signifiers unconstrained by signifieds--"Such an idea of difference punctures the mystifying notion of a transcendental signified--a signified which is said to exist positively and independently of a signifier." This writer's notion of a "transcendental signified" is, as indicated here, a positively existing referent of a sign. By bringing the signified into the system of differences, he thinks he has historicized it and rendered it neutral among those forces that direct the play of language. In this view, the human mind is free, unconstrained by a troubling determinism that recognition of an objective world entails.

But when we examine these positions we find a willful selfblinding to evidence that does not support them. For example, in Saussure's distinction between _langue_ and _parole_ we find that the two terms differ from each other in _two_ important ways: 1. The terms bear assigned meanings that are clearly different--_langue_ as system, existing independently of any speaker but only insofar as speakers exist; _parole_ as performance and existing only in the act of speech. The differences here are diametric. 2. The terms differ also ontologically, with _parole_ referring to observed human behavior and _langue_ referring to an abstract construct which is an hypothesis attempting to explain the nature of this behavior by placing it into a system of hypothesized relations. What is important to note here is that _parole_ is all that we can actually observe, while _langue_ must be inferred by means of a particular manner of observation. Clearly, once we regard these differences, it becomes obvious that statements about _parole_ must be corrigible to our actual experience and not depart from what other observers can confirm by similar observations; while statements about _langue_ need only conform to a systematic consistency among all possible statements derivable from the postulates of the theory. By absorbing the

executive features of _parole_ into the systemic structure of
_langue_, and by so doing eliminating the objective world of
signifieds, the structuralists effectively bar any appeal to
evidence from entering the grounds upon which they construct
their "system."

Even systematic consistency is not a restraining factor in
statements about _langue_, however, since the system seems
designed to absorb contradiction--not the least of which is
that the enabling factors which permit _langue_ to be thought at
all become the defining characteristics of linguistics while
_parole_ and the world of experience of which _parole_ is a part
(and the explanation of which is the ostensible reason for the
whole enterprise) is allowed to fall away as part of what the
system defines as "transcendental." (This is a peculiarly
totalitarian maneuver.) All acts of usage are "positive terms"
in statements intended to describe such acts. Since the
structuralists are motivated to circumvent subject-object
dualisms, the executive features of language are thus safely
ignored by this maneuver to historicize and neutralize them as
cultural phenomena: "An ontological substratum, a common world
of real objects, is indicated as a universal _fiction_ of
language. It is this fiction which more than anything else
reinforces our sense of the arbitrariness of the bond between
signifier and signified."[14]

What we see emerging from the structuralist and
post-structuralist program is by implication a definite
anti-science bias, and one wonders if this bias does not lie at
the heart of such theorizing. In spite of their ostensible
desire to achieve a unified humanistic field of study (if the
objective world were demonstrated to be a product of language,
then linguistics would be the roal to such a field)--an obvious
parallel to the attempt by physicists to achieve a unified
field theory--this motivation, unfortunately, tends to
disqualify such thinking. Kenneth Burke, in his _Rhetoric of
Motives_, sought in vain for a universal vocabulary that, free

from the contamination of motives itself, would be capable of examining all discourse for its underlying motives. It is an interesting and laudable goal--but highly improbable.

It is necessary at this point to observe that Saussure's concept of "difference without positive terms" applies only to signifiers and signifieds taken separately. The sound-image "father" and the sound-image "mother" are distinct from each other by virture of their differences--there is no "positive term" to which these differences point. Similarly with the "ideas" these sound-images signify; that is, the signifieds. Taken separately, the signifieds differ and these differences likewise point to no positive term. But Saussure does not rest here. A signifier and signified taken together constitute a "sign" and their combination is a "positive fact."[15]

However, at this point Saussure shifts to another strategy that enables him to maintain a "language-static" system that is internally whole and independent of a world of "transcendental signifieds." "Two signs," he argues, "each having a signified and signifier, are not different but only distinct. Between them there is only opposition. The entire mechanism of language . . . is based on oppositions . . . and on the phonic and conceptual differences they imply."[16] It is by virtue of opposition that words can be situated in linear order, or given syntagmatic relations. These oppositions are formed inside discourse. Another set of oppositions, based on similarities, and unsupported by linearity, are formed outside discourse. These are associative relations, and constitute the paradigmatic aspect of the system. Hence the familiar "syntagmatic/paradigmatic" terminology so over-used in contemporary critical discourse. The whole set of phonic and conceptual differences that constitute language is comprised of these two classes of sign co-ordination.

At the very base of this concept of the design of language in its synchronous aspect is the distinction between signifier and signified taken separately. Therefore it is to this distinction we must turn to satisfy ourselves as to the relative soundness of the whole.

With regard to Saussure's insistence on the arbitrary nature of the signifier, I don't think we can quarrel; and the concept of difference follows as a correlative quality. Since there is no natural bond between a signifier and its signified, we can only know signifiers by their differences from each other, much as the letter t depends for its identity on its being distinguishable from the other letters in the alphabet, however one wishes to style it on the page. However, does the same line of reasoning hold for the concept of signifieds taken separately? For instance, the signifiers "father" and "mother" differ from each other and as signifiers we recognize their signifieds on the basis of these differences. But what of my father and my mother, and the ideas of father and mother? Saussure holds that these too are arbitrary, that as ideas they emanate from the language system and are dependent upon their differences for their identity, not upon intrinsic qualities.

For evidence of the arbitrary nature of signifieds, Saussure adduces the fact that different native languages divide up in different ways the total field of what may be expressed in words: "One language has concepts that are absent from another," as one commentator observes. "The example which linguists like to give of such arbitrariness is that of colour terms, which vary greatly from one language to another, even though the colours themselves form a continuum and, being determined naturally by their frequency, are universal."[17]

However, it is in the nature of things that one cannot hold to the idea of arbitrariness in signifieds and at the same time illustrate it, most especially by appeal to universals! If language were arbitrary on the level of signifieds, how would we know it? Could we logically come to such a conclusion without some outside help? Even in relativistic physics the phenomena observed are not regarded as arbitrary products of mathematical description. We could recognize arbitrariness in signifieds only by reference to what is not arbitrary, and this reference would belie the assertion. Take, for example, the word "tree": "There is no property common to all trees . . . which makes it logical . . . that we should refer to them as 'trees.'"[18] The word "tree" is not derived from observation. It is a conventional signifier, just as "arbre" is. But trees, the objects, have sensible properties and these properties are what we signify by the word. Similarly with the colors mentioned above. One language may not have signifiers, and thus concepts, for all the colors in the continuum. But the signifiers they do have refer to this continuum. The fact that we can recognize variance in color concepts from one language to another implies a capacity to transcend the limitations of our native language and to devise ways within our native language to signify this broader experience. The whole thrust of science is towards reducing the illusion of arbitrariness of signifieds, which is a consequence of our partial knowledge of the systematic character of the objective world.

In Saussure's linguistics, arbitrariness and difference are correlative qualities. But the question is, are they consistently so? Consider how difference arises in the first place. When the post-structuralist Derrida argues that "the play of differences involves syntheses and referrals which prevent there from being at any moment or in any way a simple element which is present in and of itself and refers only to itself,"[19] he is in effect assigning a generative function to "play of differences," a function which Saussure's linguistics not only permits but insists on. Building on Saussure, Derrida claims that difference itself is available to perception--and thus conceptualization--because of the pressure of distance, absence, nothingness that lies between and thus gives existence to differences, much as the space between parallel lines--a nothingness in itself--makes parallelism and linearity possible. This space he calls differance and conceives as a lag or a deferral.

. . . there is no life present <u>at first</u> which would
<u>then</u> come to protect, postpone, or reserve itself
in <u>differance</u>.  The latter constitutes the essence
of life.  Or rather:  as <u>differance</u> is not an essence,
as it is not anything, it is <u>not</u> life, if Being is
determined as <u>ousia</u>, presence, essence/existence,
substance or subject . . . To defer (differer)
thus cannot mean to retard a present possibility,
to postpone an act, to put off a perception already
now possible.  That possibility is possible only
through a <u>differance</u> which must be conceived of in
other terms than those of a calculus or mechanics
of decision.  To say that <u>differance</u> is originary
is simultaneously to erase the myth of a present
origin.  Which is why "originary" must be understood as having been <u>crossed</u> <u>out</u>, without which
<u>differance</u> would be derived from an orginial
plenitude.  It is a non-origin which is originary.[20]

Derrida does not conceive this space, lag, absence, abyss,
non-origin as productive merely of mental phenomena--that is,
it is not intended by Derrida as a theory of perception; it is
regarded, rather, as the <u>source</u> of Being. As a concept it has
the virtue of being untestable, even when applied to mental
phenomena such as language, where inevitably it asserts itself:
"Even if, along with Saussure, we envisage the distinction
between signified and signifier only as the two sides of a
sheet of paper, nothing is changed.  Originary writing, if
there is one, must produce the space and the materiality of the
sheet itself."  One is locked in a logic that leads, like an
express train speeding to a precipice, directly to the
abyss--except that Derrida would reverse the image and give us
the train coming from the other direction.
       However, when one plays the logic game, one is free to
generate axioms and deduce from them all the implications they

bear. So long as one successfully avoids the corrigibility "positive terms" impose in the form of evidence, one is free to play on _ad infinitum_. Let us play our own game and select concepts of _chance_ and _necessity_, and argue for these as fundamental generative processes.

According to our game, the interactions of chance and necessity give rise to Being, ourselves included. It is out of their interaction that individuality, and thus distinctiveness, arise in phenomena (or in signifieds, to use structuralist terms). Here is an example gameplan: Consider pebbles washing downstream. The physical laws which determine the dynamics of flow, inertia, gravity, etc., constitutes the necessity of pebbles washing downstream, and from the operation of these laws we can predict the _fact_ of washing and the consequent wear this would cause of the pebbles. But the distance washed and the actual shape of any particular pebble are not deducible from these laws--any more than a particular organism is deducible from the laws of biological evolution--and are therefore unpredictable. Distance and shape are _products_ _of_ _chance_.

To learn the facts of the particular, one must observe actual pebbles. From this view, it is easy to see that _differences_ between them are _not_ equally products of chance, a chance which operates on each pebble separately at every moment of its existence and thus generates its particularity _in_ every moment. In our logic, chance does not generate _differences_; these are mental phenomena produced by observation. What chance generates is the particularities that constitute the individuality of the pebbles. Once understood as a mental phenomenon, _difference_ itself can be seen as derivative and as a sign, not only of the invisible force of chance, but of individuality and presence. Hence, _difference_ becomes an indicator of a world of "positive terms" or "transcendental signifieds." Even on the level of quantum mechanics, where the ghostly dances of ephemera energize the material world, chance and necessity operate in their detectable fashion.

According to our logic game, which strikes me as more consistent with experience than Derrida's, particularity is a character stamped on all things, a positive presence-in-itself. Derrida can be reduced to arguing that at best we _perceive_ particularity by "syntheses and referrals" as it were; that it is only in our _knowing_ that a particularity depends upon difference. But this would remove the force and point of his argument. Accordingly, we can claim that since it is only on "presences" that chance can operate, we can argue much more soundly than the deconstructionists the opposite that the field of signifieds is anything _but_ arbitrary.

The fundamental power of all mentality, whether human or animal, consists in the capacity to sort particulars into categories based on similarities and differences. That animals have been demonstrated to have this capacity is a sign that it is pre-linguistic. Once we establish the concrete and particular nature of the field of signifieds, or at least that portion of it which is sensible, we can quickly see how easily we can translate thousands of bits of linguistic information into alternative linguistic systems with little ambiguity and loss.

When Saussure argues, for example, that "if words stood for pre-existing concepts, they would all have exact equivalents in meaning from one language to the next; but this is not true," he uses as examples _louer_ _une_ _maison_ (to let a house) and the German _mieten_ and _vermieten_. These are words for actions, words for doings--which we may _expect_ to be different for different cultures. But what of the word "house" or words that signify sensible objects? In the case of a word like "house," the physical object may acquire different values and intensities for different language groups, and these shadings may not be translatable or even comprehensible to those who do not share the particular environment, customs and world view that give rise to these nuances. But these differences are emotional not linguistic and not only can be but frequently are bridged by those individuals who acquire native fluency in more than one language. Our awareness of the existence of these nuances could not otherwise have been attained.

That the worlds conceptualized by two different languages can be bridged by a single knower indicates that many signifiers in each language point to signifieds existing independently of language and available to all language. The relationships between sensation, perception and conceptualization (this last the process in which language functions fully as the medium of actualization) are left completely unexplored not only by Saussure but by structuralists and post-structuralists thinkers generally and by literary critics who wave structuralist paradoxes in the faces of their consternated brethren.

To the notion that the realm of signifieds is a fiction--"from the point of view of language an ontological substratum, a common world of real objects, is indicated as a universal fiction of language. It is this fiction which more than anything else reinforces our sense of the arbitrariness of the bond between signifier and signified"--I must, like Dr. Johnson, kick the stone and insist that my experience of the world is a different thing from how I speak about this experience. For instance, let a man thoroughly familiar with the signifier "tiger" assert that its signified is an emanation from language, and thus a "fiction," try to convince himself of the adequacy of his statement in the jaws of the beast.

That the signifier is arbitrary in its relation to what it signifies is mere common sense--only a kabbalist would argue for a natural relationship between the two. But to move from arbitrariness on this level to the view that language is a system of signs whose signifieds emanate from language itself has no logical warrant or evidential basis.

Saussure's _Course in General Linguistics_ cannot be faulted for the extremes to which contemporary writers have pushed its ideas. Much of genuine value has emerged from linguistics and Saussure's work can rightly be regarded as innovative. What I regard as weaknesses in his thought are important here not for the purposes of criticism of Saussure, but for the later radicalism that these weaknesses have spawned in what we call the structuralist and post-structuralist movements. The concepts of difference and arbitrariness have become axioms in a school of thought that has become exceedingly powerful--both for what it says and for the reactions it has provoked. Today, it is almost impossible to discuss a "literary" work; one must, instead, recognize the work as _text_, i.e., as a use of signs not in essence different from their use in a menu. The "author" is widely regarded as an instrument through whom language expresses itself in one vast textuality, of which individual texts are manifestations. The "reader" is transformed into a set of rules and renamed "reading-as-such," and Man is transformed into an illusion "engendered by the play of language." In this new age, one either writes or is written--in either case, individual consciousness does not exist.[21]

In regard to this last assumption, that individual mentality is a mere vessel or instrument of language and hence not finally in possession of itself, one would have thought that our century-long and acrimonious debate on behaviorist psychology would have exerted at least some moderating influence on the facility with which a Jonathan Culler, for example, argues away human consciousness: "A text can be read only in relation to other texts, and it is made possible by the codes which animate the discursive space of a culture . . . . The work is a product not of a biographically defined individual . . . but of writing itself."[22]

In the discussion response to his essay, "Structure, Sign, and Play," delivered at the Johns Hopkins symposium, The

languages of Criticism and the Sciences of Man,[23] Jacques
Derrida responds to a question put by Serge Doubrovsky on the
problem of perception which arises if one argues that the realm
of signifieds is not centered in a field exterior to
consciousness:

> I should say that once I recognized (perception)
> as a necessary conservation. Now I don't know
> what perception is and I don't believe that
> anything like perception exists. Perception
> is precisely a concept, a concept of an
> intuition or of a given originating from
> the thing itself, present itself in its
> meaning, independently from language, from
> the system of reference. And I believe that
> perception is interdependent with the concept
> of origin and of center and consequently what-
> ever strikes at the meta-physics of which I
> have spoken strikes also at the very concept
> of perception. I don't believe that there is
> any perception.[24]

Derrida is at least consistent and willing to recognize
the consequences of his position. I quote at length here
because we come near to what I regard as the essential
motivations underlying Derrida's thought. Employing Saussurian
techniques, Derrida claims that the signified to which the
signifier "perception" points is a concept--not the experience
of perception, the physiological and psychological complex that
results in a content of awareness achieving definition as
itself--and as such suffers the fate of all concepts
constituting the metaphysical tradition of Western
Civilization. In "Structure, Sign, and Play," Derrida argues
that the idea of presence--the notion of a world of objects
"out there," existing independently of human mentality--is a

product of our tradition of metaphysical thought and in actuality is an illusion. His analysis of the illusion of presence depends essentially on the Saussurian concepts we have already examined--difference and arbitrariness. In an audacious display of circular reasoning, Derrida argues that "the absence of the transcendental signified extends the domain and the interplay of signification ad infinitum," because "in the absence of a center or origin (presence), everything becomes discourse." Everything becomes discourse because "the central signified, the original or transcendental signified, is never absolutely present outside a system of differences."[25]

Central to Derrida's logic here is a theory of perception which conceives of the mind's perceptual activity as playing no role in the trace left by an external stimulus on the memory. In his essay, "Freud and the Scene of Writing," he analyzes Freud's metaphor of the Mystic Writing Pad as a model of the relations between the perceptual neurons, consciousness, memory, and the unconscious. Derrida discusses this metaphor in terms of how the Freudian model serves to illustrate the applicability of his deconstructive concepts--the problem of perception playing a key role in the analysis. What emerges is a model of perception consistent with Derrida's philosophy.

The mystic writing pad is the child's toy on which one engraves over a clear plastic or cellophane sheet and leaves an impression on an opaque underlying sheet produced by a dark wax base which underlies all. Consciousness is represented by the opaque sheet which receives an impression from memory (the dark wax) when a stimulus is applied to the clear overlying sheet (the perceptual neurons). Being is, of course, the active force which engraves. Consciousness is a passive field, an interface, between the unconsciousness and Being upon which "dead" representations of the "trace" of Being are manifested. The "life" of these traces, or what life there is, takes place in the dark below. What appears in consciousness is a "representation," an image with no substance--the living dead.

Perceptual activity is, as in this model, a transparent or neutral medium through which a trace passes, but which retains no influence of the trace and remains unaltered: always virgin.

The extent to which this model is inconsistent with observable experience is easy to demonstrate. When I look up and notice an airplane at a very high altitude, what I in fact see is a cross-shaped speck. Nevertheless, if anyone should ask me what I see, I would not say "a speck" but "an airplane." What I see is a speck; what I perceive is a plane. Whence comes the plane? Obviously, the plane is not produced in my consciousness at the end of a period of "sortings and referrals"; I perceive the plane directly as a plane. Yet if someone who had never heard of airplanes, never had seen one before, should be standing beside me, he would not "see" a plane upon noticing the same speck. What the example suggests is that perception is an active, inference making process inseparable from consciousness and memory and partaking of the nature of both simultaneously--a model which is not just at odds with that in the metaphor of the mystic writing pad; but a model which requires a fundamental alteration in the conception of the nature of human thought and of Being embodied in the metaphor itself.[26] Clearly, some part of the perception and memory interact in and partake of consciousness, as the example suggests, to produce the awareness of the world necessary for our acting in it--for the purposes of our survival, at the very least.

However, one must take only a very short step to apply Derrida's deconstructionist philosophy and its subordinate concepts to literary criticism. Once the post-structuralist achieves the "abysm"--the notion of language as a decentered system of signifiers--the task of conceiving literary works in such a way as to skirt the host of critical problems that emerged from early twentieth-century critical activity becomes relatively easy. Conceiving the text as a "play" of signifiers that can go on ad infinitum "allows no enunciative subject to hold the position of judge, teacher, analyst, confessor, or decoder. The theory of the Text can coincide only with the activity of writing."[27] What the critic can do is deconstruct the text--that is, work through "the structured geneology of its concepts in the most scrupulous fashion, from within, but at the same time from a certain external perspective which [he] cannot name or describe."[28]

This activity enables us to determine what the history of concepts conceals from, forbids to, or opens up to thought.[29] This "textual activity" and its product gives pleasure (a certain need to justify the activity seems to be felt here--we never get completely beyond tradition, it seems). The concept of "play" is especially important, however, for literary texts do not generally offer us "knowledge" as philosophical and scientific texts do--though what post-structuralists mean by the word "knowledge" must be qualified by their view of "decentering." Here is Roland Barthes clarifying the idea of play:

> In fact, reading in the sense of consuming (reading casually for cultural meanings of a text) is not playing with the Text. Here "playing" must be understood in all its polysemy. The Text itself plays (like a door on its hinges, like the device in which there is some "play"); and the reader himself plays twice over: playing the Text as one plays a game, he searches for a practice that will re-produce the Text; but, to keep that practice from being reduced to a passive, inner mimesis (the Text being precisely what resists such a reduction), he also plays the Text in the musical sense of the term.[30]

However one "plays" a text, I would like to come back to Derrida's notion of "deconstructing" the text in order to "displace or undo the most fundamental categories of our intellectual life."[31]

Suppose our writers and teachers became "deconstructionists" of the Derridean persuasion. What would result? Would we enter a period of stasis creatively? This is the present danger, because the intellectual horizon of Derrida's imaginative mode is bounded by already existing texts, and in a sense is parasitic upon them. If every time someone entertained a thought, and by habit of mind "deconstructed" it into its fundamental categories in order to displace these categories or undo them to determine their historicity within a system of differences, no new thinking would or could take place. Clearly, Derrida's "post-structuralism" is an all-consuming analytic methodology incapable itself of originating texts upon which it can function as a critical activity--a condition not generic to critical activity as such--and depends upon the synthetic imaginative habits of mind that, disregarding the manner by which language works in the production of thought, concentrates its efforts on system building; whether the systems be those of philosophy, science, literature, politics, or popular entertainment.

As a philosopher, Derrida's deconstructive efforts have been aimed primarily at philosophical texts, but his efforts are emulated by literary critics who find in him a way out of the so-called impasse of criticism-as-handmaiden-to-literature. But what these critics fail to see, however, is that in order to "displace or undo" the "fundamental categories" of intellectual life, these categories must first be synthesized and brought into a coherent system of thought by someone. It is in this work that Wordsworth found "Reason in its most exalted mood," and it is this work which is responsible for the production of texts that Derrida would deconstruct.

Thus when Derrida argues that meaning can be explained by an underlying system of differences and that our sense of the

self as an originating and controlling consciousness is a mere
illusion produced by the mataphysical tradition of "presence,"
he is in effect implying a pair of opposing categories of mental
power. These categories are the analytical and, for lack of a
better term, the systemic. The opposition--analytic/systemic--
has the peculiar property of opposing the element of will to
non-will such that all activities that are not analytic are the
consequences of the operation of systems upon a willess  mind.

These systems are what comprise the intellectual and
cultural heritage of mankind and, in effect, think themselves
through history into the forms they have achieved at any
particuar time: "To put it very schematically," Jonathan Culler
explains, "in each of these fields (psychoanalysis after Lacan,
linguistics after Saussure, and anthropology after
Levy-Strauss), arguments citing in some way the priority of
difference have made the subject something constituted by or
resulting from the play of systems rather than a controlling
consciousness which is the master and ultimate origin of
systems."[32]

Thus, the analytic power of mind, in stepping outside of
these systems in order to deconstruct them, becomes the only
arena wherein the critic can exercise his will. It is on the
basis of this "will" that the post-structuralist can claim a
priority for his work over that of the systems upon which it is
based. The maneuver has the double advantage of elevating the
critical work above the systems that comprise the heritage it
deconstructs and of rendering it immune to a similar
deconstruction. The opposition between the analytic and
systemic powers is, though always implied and never attested to
explicity in post-structuralist thought, a necessary one because
if on the one hand the analytic were itself absorbed into the
systemic, the whole of human intellectual history would become
at one stroke beyond criticism. It is only the capacity to
deflect our thought backward so to speak from a vantage under
the control of a non-systemic aspect of mind that the problem of

illusion can be perceived and the historicity of intellectual categories observed.

On the other hand, if the systemic were absorbed into the dominion of human will, the whole epistemology by which the analytic is protected and privileged--that "meaning is based on underlying systems of differences" the play of which constitutes the thinking subject--would evaporate into the thin airs of inconsequence. Thus the deflection of thought in the analytic mode becomes the only ground of human freedom. To preserve this ground it is necessary that the analytic method uncover no other and competing ground of freedom in the operation of the human mind. To avoid an utter and inescapable determinism, a determinism that would soon swallow this ground of freedom, the post-structuralists posit a totally free play of differences in the systems that comprise the heritage.

Ultimately, this free play of differences is conceived as the generative father of our myths, languages, the unconscious, societal rules, the structures of literature, the episteme of a given historical period, etc. All of these are the systems that constitute a heritage.

By a peculiar paradox or twist of logic, this "free play of differences" is placed beyond the control of the living human subject who is made the non-willing ground of their play. We have already seen why this maneuver is necessary. It seems to me that, from the point of view of the Derrideans, a highly undesirable implication arises from this analytic/systemic opposition.

There must, of necessity, be two kinds of meaning--namely, undeconstructed and deconstructed. ' The validity of undeconstructed meanings can be tested by the fruits they bear in actual experience, whereas it is in the nature of things that deconstructed meanings are always hypostatic. Thus, as an excercise of intellectual will, post-structuralist thought must remain, as pointed out on several occasions above, forever beyond the pale of evidential discourse--a consequence that at the least may guarantee its perpetuity but which renders it, at the same time, a member of that category Coleridge named: professorial ectoplasm.

This is a bind created by post-structuralist premises, for if it were possible to acquire actual evidence for a deconstructed meaning, the evidence itself would constitute a determinism in the relations held as "free play" and at once render meaning necessary and nullify the concept of "free play." Evidence of a deconstructed meaning is in short impossible, for evidence as such would invalidate the premises upon which deconstruction of meanings is based. It is because of the problems evidential discourse gives rise to that Derrideans must insist on Saussure's concept of "differences without positive terms." So understood, when signifiers are said to correspond to concepts, we must realize "that the concepts are purely differential and defined not by their positive content but negatively by their relations with other terms of the system." The virtue of this position is that it disqualifies the appeal to evidence and undercuts the value of evidence in its role as a check on thought. The dangers contingent upon such a method of philosophizing are evident, if I may be excused the pun. There is no way within the premises established by post-structuralist thought to counter or disprove any conclusion. So long as the Derrideans contend that the writer or speaker (the user of language) is blind to the statement of his text, the Derrideans will always be able to point out this statement to him. One can only check the critic's accuracy by using the critic's method--which will of course yield the same result. It is a no-win situation for all but the critic.

These are the underlying motives that give rise to the strategies of post-structuralist thought. The privileging of the analytic in the implied analytic/systemic opposition is a neat little bit of self-serving, and as such necessarily casts suspicion upon the whole enterprise. But one last criticism before closing this chapter.

Here is an analogy to help understand the logical consequences of post-structuralist thought: We install gyroscopes to help an airship's instrumentation monitor its orientation with regard to a vertical and horizontal axis. When these scopes work, the stability of the ship can be maintained automatically by continuous adjustments in flight attitude based on the information provided by the scopes. Now, is there any meaningful sense in which one can argue that this stability is an illusion, a false stability, a mere simulacrum of a pure ideality--stability-in-itself--which exists only as a phenomenon of a system of signs that generate meaning by virtue of differences among them? Since Stabilility-in-itself has no positive term, no signified in an objectivity external to signs, it cannot be the ground or "center that is elsewhere," i.e., external to the system of signs, that the Derrideans contend must exist to be the dictating referent that would give determinate meaning to the system's sense of stability.

The analogy is more subtle than it appears at first, for the gyroscopes send "signals" to the monitoring equipment which, in effect, interprets them as corrections in flap and rudder positions, for the sake of a "stability" it construes as a particular orientation--and no other--on x and y axes. To argue here that the system is mechanical is beside the point, for we built it and it functions as we want it to. Furthermore, it functions on the model of human sensations, and interpretation of these signals. The problem of a Stability-in-itself can never arise because the system that senses and signals, receives, interprets and acts on the basis of these signals is not self-conscious and capable of questioning the "authority" of the information generated by the system's workings.

Let us, then, add the ingredient of self-consciousness together with a dispositon to raise such questions. What would result? Indisputably, it would fail and the plane crash. It would fail, be it noted, not because of the added ingredient of self-consciousness but because of its tendency to doubt the authority of positive terms to its signals. It need not be pointed out that, were people generally to adopt the post-structuralist's epistemology and view of language, the analogy would hold to the end. And let us not pretend that the signals sent by the gyroscopes and acted upon by other mechanisms bear no relation to human language. They are unambiguous, admitted, having a one-to-one correspondence between sign and referent, etc. The fact remains, they are a language of our own devising, a product of our intelligence, coming into being through the mediation of our awareness and language. Infinitely more subtle languages exist by which we "talk" to ships millions of miles away that respond to us. Ambiguity and slippage in referentiation, irony and so forth, may be characteristics of human language, but the question remains as to whether they are defining characteristics or the result of strategies of usage and, simply enough, error.

NOTES

[1]Northrop Frye, <u>Anatomy</u> <u>of</u> <u>Criticism</u> (New York:    Atheneum, 1969), p. 11.

[2]Frye, p. 11.

[3]See Jacques Derrida, "Structure, Sign, and Play," in <u>The</u> <u>Languages</u> <u>of</u> <u>Criticism</u> <u>and</u> <u>the</u> <u>Sciences</u> <u>of</u> <u>Man</u>. eds., Richard Macksey and Eugenio Donato (Baltimore:    The Johns Hopkins Press, 1970), pp. 247-72.    Derrida argues, persuasively according to some, that the concept of structure always depended upon a process of giving it a center or referring it to a point of presence.    This dependency of structure upon a center or presence is as old as Western philosophy itself--"one cannot in fact conceive of an unorganized structure" (p. 247)--and it was the function of this center not only to orient, balance, and organize the structure but "above all to make sure that the organizing principle of the structure would limit what we might call the <u>freeplay</u> of the structure" (p. 247).    This concept of a center or presence to structure, without which structure would be unthinkable, is the consequence of a "desire" to be free from anxiety caused by uncertainty.    But a moment in Western philosophy--Derrida attributes this moment to Nietzsche--came when it became necessary to "think" this center; to supply, as it were, a mental locus to satisfy this desire.    "This moment was that in which language invaded the universal problematic." The centering of structure, Derrida argues, was never a

consequence of perception--he argues that there is no perception--but was the consequence of a desire fulfilled by the processes of signification. However, since our discovery that there is no "transcendental or privileged signified" (no presence to which a signifier points outside the system of differences that comprises language) the domain and the interplay of signification became extended ad infinitum. Thus structure (or the structurality of structure) has become decentered. In this view, the question of how concepts originate, how a "world view" or "metaphysics" became elaborated over time can only be answered by the proposition that "language speaks itself."

[4] Frank Lentricchia, After the New Criticism (Chicago: University of Chicago Press, 1980), p. 112. Lentricchia discusses the problematic nature of the Course in General Linguistics at some length and I agree with his contention that however uncertain we may be about some of the details of Saussure's great work, his central ideas are so innovative as to put their authorship above all controversey.

[5] Lentricchia, p. 112.

[6] Lentricchia, p. 113.

[7] Lentricchia, p. 113 and note 33.

[8] For an excellent summary discussion of the Anglo-American concept of structure, see Arthur Berndtson, Art, Expression, and Beauty (Chicago: Holt, Rinehart and Winston, Inc., 1969), pp. 41-56. For all the theoretical work done under the rubrics of "structuralism" and "post-structuralism," the concept of structure itself is seldom elaborated and remains an undefined term in contemporary critical theory, where such substitutions as "structurization," "structurality," "structure-in-itself,"

"deconstruction," etc. are used and defined in paradoxical terms against the unexamined "common sense" meaning of "structure" (see note 3 above, where the term "structure" is left undefined in an elaborate analysis of the meanings of the terms "center" and "presence"). According to Jonathan Culler in _Structuralist Poetics_ (New York: Cornell University Press, 1975), a work "has structure and meaning because it is read in a certain way, because these potential properties, latent in the object itself, are actualized by the theory of discourse applied in the act of reading" but according to Lentricchia, "theoretical consistency would require that Culler say that structure is latent in the reader, not the object" (pp. 107-08). The shifting of attention from a consideration of structure to a consideration of "structurization" or "structure-in-itself" has served primarily to obfuscate, since attention is continuously shifted from "works that have structure" to a set of ideological determinants that remain in constant flux--and hence never achieve the status of determinants at all. It is obvious, for example, that structure exists on different levels and has different sources.

Any literary work is literary first and foremost because it uses language as its medium. So in a fundamental sense, literary structures consist of the structures that make language available as language. But these structures do not exhaust what we identify as the structures of poems and fictions. In a sense one may say that the _structures_ of language are what comprise the literary medium rather than saying language itself does so. These structures--together with other kinds of structures--are then taken into, shaped into, literary structures which comprise the literariness and individuality of works. How conventions arise and spead out into a reading public to pattern reader expectations is a process scholars may in time disclose to our satisfaction. For now, it is enough to observe that these language structures do not by themselves exhaust the structures that exist in a literary work.

There are also logical structures, especially those that
govern identity, implication, conjunction, disjunction, and
the forms of relatedness such as smaller than, greater than and
equal to. These are structures which are essentially
non-linguistic and which govern relationships among the
parts--it is partly from these structures that meaning emerges,
just as meaning emerges from them in mathmatical discourse.
The structures of language serve to make specifically literary
discourse available to our understanding, while the logical
structures serve, in part, to help define the uniqueness of the
specific text. For example, in Hopkins's "The Windhover," the
lines:

> Brute beauty and valor and act, oh, air, pride, plume here
> Buckle! AND the fire that breaks from thee then, a billion
> Times told lovelier, more dangerous, O my chevalier!

are manipulations of the logical categories of conjunction,
equal to, greater than, and implication serving to establish an
identity.

Similarly, Yeats' lines:

> Before me floats an image, man or shade,
> Shade more than man, more image than a shade

are manipulations of the logical categories of disjunction and
greater than serving as in Hopkins' lines to establish an
identity. In both cases, the logical structures are expressed
as syntax and thus in language structures, but as logical
structures they can be expressed in the non-linguistic medium
of symbolic logic and thus recognized as independent of verbal
language. These logical structures are also matter available
to the writer to make use of in literary composition. The
writer does not invent these categories of structures and he is

not free to write without them, insofar as meaning is
conditioned by them and cannot exist independently of them. In
a sense then it is correct to say that the writer is
constrained by them if he would write, but false to conclude
therefore that the writer is determined by them. The
structures of concrete, wood, steel, clay, etc., each coerce
the builder that would construct with them to build in certain
ways and they limit the kind of structures he would end up
with. But within these limitations, and by willingly abiding
by them, he can, and in fact does, create new forms.

The argument as to whether literary structure is latent
within the reader and is "actualized by the theory of
discourse applied in the act of reading" or externally there in
the work and coercive, is thus seen to be a distinction without a
difference. The Cartesian distinction between subject and
object does not apply to the question of literary structures.
Insofar as language norms and logic hold in a culture, our
minds which function as minds because of them participate in a
common identity-establishing property without which they could
not exist at all.

Thus language and logic are universal within the community
that is defined by them and exist simultaneously in each of us
and independently of each of us. In this there is no mystery.
But again, these categories of structure do not exhaust the
levels of structures that exist in a literary work, though they
function as guarantors of communication on the most elementary
level. To these must be added now the specifically literary
structures that define the discourse and distinguish it from
other kinds. Such structures as metaphor, simile, metonomy,
synecdoche, and the whole variety of tropes and figures and
rhetorical devices are composed of the structures of language
and logic. Their invention is peculiar to literary discourse
though not exclusive to it. And to these must be added the
structures of prosody--meter, rhyme, stanzaic form, as well as
literary type. It is only in regard to these, what we may call

macro-structures, that we enter the world of literature. Even though these structures impose limitations upon the writer, they are so numerous and interact in such an infinite variety of ways that the writer is essentially free within them to compose as he wills. The mistake is to confuse limitations with determinism. There is no human activity that is free of limitations. What is important to recognize is that what limitations we choose to reside in determine the kind of our activity but not the activity itself. This is a distinction, simple as it is, which seems to elude the critical determinist.

[9]Lentricchia, p. 114 and note 35.

[10]Ferdinand De Saussure, Course in General Linguistics (New York: Philosophical Library, 1959), pp. 116-17.

[11]Saussure, p. 118. Of the sign considered in its totality, Saussure observes that "difference generally implies positive terms between which the difference is set up; but in language there are only differences without positive terms." By "intrinsic value," Saussure means referentiation, or more precisely, the traditional view of a word's non-linguistic meaning: "Whether we take the signified or the signifier, language has neither ideas or sounds that existed before the linguistic system, but only conceptual and phonic differences that have issued from the system" (p. 120).

[12]Lentricchia, p. 116 and note 41.

[13]Lentricchia, p. 123. Mr. Lentricchia's language is most amusing. He postures in it to the extent that he would have us believe that people generally already accept the contention that no objective reality exists and find mystifying the archaic belief in objects, objectivity, external reality or "transcendental signifieds," this last term devised to conceal

the real meaning and thrust of post-structuralist
principles--"transcendental" in this context (the Derridean)
means not "concerned with the a priori, minimizing the
importance of experience," but refers to the world of sense
experience itself, a reversal which ought to put us on guard
and to which we ought rightly to object.

[14]Lentricchia, p. 119. Underscoring mine.

[15]Saussure, p. 120.

[16]Saussure, p. 121.

[17]John Sturrock, "Introduction," Structuralism and Since:
From Levy-Strauss to Derrida (New York: Oxford University
Press, 1979), p. 9.

[18]Sturrock, p. 9.

[19]Jonathan Culler, "Jacques Derrida," in Structuralism and
Since, p. 164.

[20]Jacques Derrida, "Freud and the Scene of Writing," in
Writing and Difference (Chicago: University of Chicago Press,
1978), p. 203. Italics in the text.

[21]For an excellent contrast between the features of the
traditional or humanistic paradigm of the writing and reading
of literature and those of our present critical practice, see
M. H. Abrams, "How to Do Things With Texts," Partisan Review,
56 (1981), 566-88.

[22]Culler, Pursuit of Signs (Ithaca, New York: Cornell
University Press, 1981), p. 38.

[23]See note 3 above for a brief discussion of Derrida's
main argument in "structure, Sign, and Play."

[24]Macksey and Donato, p. 272.

[25]Macksey and Donato, p. 249.

[26]See Brand Blanshard on perception in "Reply to Errol E. Harris, 'Blanshard on Perception and Free Ideas,'" passim, The Philosophy of Brand Blanshard (La Salle, Illinois: Open Court, 1980).

[27]Roland Barthes, "From Work to Text," in Textual Strategies: Perspectives in Post-Structuralist Criticism, ed., Josue V. Harari (Ithaca, New York: Cornell University Press, 1979), p. 81.

[28]Jacques Derrida, quoted in Culler, "Jacques Derrida," in Structuralism and Since, p. 179.

[29]The following is a passage from Joseph Riddel, "Decentering the Image," in Textual Strategies, p. 324. The essay itself is an excellent example of the application of Derridean methodology and the passage in question illustrates the kind of observation it inspires: "From Emerson to (Charles) Olson, there is not a straight line but a movement of appropriations, of decenterings, of repetitions that manage to keep the possibility of an 'American' poetry open" (underscoring mine). The statement implies a number of assumptions about writing, about poetry, about historical process as it affects literature, poetry, the writer which are enabled by the Derridean post-structuralist notions we have been examining. First, it implies that a historical process (taking place in language) is determinative in such a way that it can "open" or "close" the very possibility of creative activity in the present. I believe experience teaches that this is wholly wrong. One is compelled to ask Mr. Riddel if such a process has ever "closed" the possibility of poetry--and

how he would have known about it. Riddel's statement implies an
authority over the present in the form of tradition that is
absolute and deterministic, whereas the tradition can ever
only provide possibilities--positives never negatives. Logic
alone should have cautioned him. However, the concept of
creativity suggested by Riddel is such that its generative
powers are conceived as limited, shaped, and controlled by the
past; I might suggest that this concept of creativity is all
that post-stucturalist thought will or can allow to it. Sanity
and experience compel one to observe, however, that only the
resources, agitations, conditions of the present can ever
limit the creative moment. Riddel, following Derrida, wrongly
supposes that the shapes, developments, events of the literary
tradition are objective and absolute (when Derrida discovers
the "illusion" of "center" or "presence" in Western thought, he
is an absolutist in applying the concept to the
"deconstruction" of texts), that what the tradition is for one
it is for everyone. Again, this is contrary to experience.
Long ago, Eliot taught us that the tradition is never static,
that is, conceived in the same way by great writers--this is
why they change the tradition with their own productions. Each
writer shapes his own tradition--thus it is impossible to say
that one conception of literary historical process "opens" or
"closes" possibilities.

[30]Barthes, p. 79.

[31]Culler, "Jacques Derrida, " in Structuralism and Since,
p. 179.

[32]Culler, "Jacques Derrida," in Structuralism and Since,
p. 174.

CHAPTER 3

THE FACE THAT GAZES BACK:
MARXIST LITERARY CRITICISM


My viewpoint, according to which the economic
development and formation of a society appears
as a process of natural history, is less able
than any other to render the individual responsible for the relations of which he remains
socially the creation.

(Karl Marx, Das Kapital)


A dialectics that moves from the objective to
the objective, turning the subjective into a
passing and inessential moment, is a pseudo-
dialectics whose phraseology is merely failing
to conceal what is in reality a return to a
naturalistic causality.

(Serge Doubrovsky, The New
Criticism in France)

Unlike the psychoanalytic and the post-structuralist
critical theories, Marxist literary theory is grounded in the
concept of a material world that is reflected in literature.
How the Marxist achieves his concept of the material world and
what he means by the reflection of this world in literature,
however, is another thing--certainly, he does not mean the
common sense notion of these things. The concept of history as
a becoming played out not in but as human consciousness is
essential to all Marxist theorizing--in politics, sociology,
aesthetics.

We may, very abstractly, consider the psychoanalytic and
post-structuralist theses as regarding human consciousness

either as an active, adapting agency or as a passive agency upon which Being actively engraves its traces. For Marx this conflict in the concept of the nature of mind--which in various forms has a venerable history of its own--is not a question of theory; it is a practical question: "The truth, i.e., the reality and power, of thought must be demonstrated in practice. The contest as to the reality or non-reality of a thought which is isolated from practice, is a purely scholastic question . . . . Philosophers have only interpreted the world in various ways, but the real task is to alter it."[1]  For Marx, the subject and object, both the knower and the thing known, modify each other in a continual process of mutual adaptation. Marx calls this process "dialectical" because it is never fully completed.

The material world is a product of this dialectics and as such is at least in part mind-dependent. The practical, for Marx, then, is a question as to what kind of world shall emerge from the process of the dialectic. This is where his philosophy of history enters his general metaphysics. In later Marxist theory the practical question dominates in the form of the concept of historical determinism, the end product of which is the great alteration known as the Socialist State. Marxist literary theory conceives its activity as essentially a "service" to this great task of altering the world. It is in the context of the problem to which this idea of and committment to serving gives rise that Marxist literary theory must be evaluated.

As a way into our discussion, then, let me begin with an obvious and amusing bit of "serving" that will illustrate the dimensions of the problem. What follows is a passage from Frederick Jameson's Marxism and Form, in which the author rhapsodizes over a Marxist analysis by T. W. Adorno of why the Vienese excel in music.

Let the following passage from Adorno's Philosophy of the New Music stand, therefore, not so much as

an implied philosophical proposition, or as a
novel reinterpretation of the historical phenomena
in question, but rather as a metaphorical composition, a kind of stylistic or rhetorical trope
through which the new historical and dialectical
consciousness, shattering the syntactic conventions
of older analytical or static thought, comes to its
truth in the language of events:

> It is hardly an accident that mathematical
> techniques in music as well as logical posi-
> tivism originated in Vienna. The fondness for
> number games is as peculiar to the Viennese mind
> as the game of chess in the coffee house. There
> are social reasons for it. All the while
> intellectually productive forces in Austria
> were rising to the technical level characteristic
> of high capitalism, material forces lagged behind.
> The resultant unused capacity for figures became
> the symbolic fulfillment of the Viennese intellectual.
> If he wanted to take part in the actual process of
> material production, he had to look for a position
> in Imperial Germany. If he stayed home, he became
> a doctor or a lawyer or clung to number games as a
> mirage of financial power. Such is the way the
> Viennese intellectual tries to prove something
> to himself, and--bitte schon!--to everyone else
> as well.

Psychoanalysis of the Austrian character? Object
lesson in the way society resolves in the imaginary
realm those contradictions which it cannot overcome
in the real? Stylistic juxtapositon of music,
symbolic logic, and financial sheets? The text
under consideration is all of these things, but

it is first and foremost a complete thing, I am
tempted to say a poetic object. For its most
characteristic connectives ("it is no accident")
are less signs of some syllogistic operation to
perform than they are equivalents of the "just
as . . . so" of the heroic simile.[2]

Is Jameson's almost ecstatic response to Adorno's little piece
of analysis justified? He sees it, he is "tempted to say" as a
poetic object. If indeed any analysis achieved this status
while being at the same time a philosophical proposition, a
novel reinterpretation of phenomena, AND a metaphorical
composition of such stylistic and rhetorical perfection as to
provoke us into a new historical and dialectical consciousness
while shattering the syntactic conventions of older analytical
or static thought to achieve truth in the language of
events--we all would abase ourselves, most humbly, in the
presence of the achievement, for it would be a break-through in
human thought and expression of evolutionary proportions. Let
us see if the Adorno passage deserves such self-abasement on
our part, and let us begin by asking what Adorno's point is in
the analysis.

It seems to me that what Adorno is saying can be put,
fairly, in the following terms: a. The Viennese are fond of
number games because, b. intellectual growth outpaced material
growth in their country and, c. this resulted in the Viennese
playing number games in order to compensate for their lack of
capital, which compensation, d. proved to themselves
"something"--presumably that they could deal with the real
world if they had a chance. (I would ask the reader to compare
my abstract with the original to assure himself I did not leave
anything out.) Clearly this analysis is meant to illustrate
the Marxist principle of the modes of production determining
the cultural expression of the time. What shall we say of this
analysis?

Does it read like journalism? Does it read like good journalism? Adorno is no journalist, but observe the typical logic of this everyday journalese--the writer identifies a motive (in this case wish-fulfillment) on the part of a possible member of a class (Viennese musicians), and then distributes this characteristic among all members of the class (with no exceptions noted, since this would cost him his case). We may further question the wish-fulfillment motive he attributes to his class. The idea of compensation is one of the most general of Freudian concepts and therefore the easiest to apply to behavior--and for this reason it is the Freudian concept most frequently abused by analysts from other disciplines. Thus we see the extension fallacy manipulated in the interest of distributing that most banal and superficial of human characteristics among members of a class in order to account for the Viennese excellence in musical composition.

That the logic is fallacious can be seen at a glance. It is not even plausible. As a psychoanalysis, a professional in that discipline would wince to see it. What of its writing--does its style shatter the syntactic conventions of older analytical or static thought? I see here nothing but serviceable prose, competent to be sure, but nothing more. The phrase "It is hardly an accident that," so far from being a metaphorical indicator--a prose equivalent to the "just as . . . so" convention of the heroic simile--is a typical linguistic evasion, as old as language itself, serving the purposes of insinuation without intellectual responsibility or accountability. We see it used most frequently in the smear campaign. However, I won't tire the reader further with a formal analysis of the passage's style. Truth? Yes--to the Marxist, for whom every aspect of human character can be explained in terms of economic order. To the Non-Marxist the analysis is just plain silly.

Can we glimpse the working of a new historical and dialectical consciousness in the passage? I find this claim particularly embarrassing and frustrating to argue against, for there is an element of truth to it. The answer is yes, obviously! Insofar as we may regard Marxism as new and dialectical and its philosophy of historical process as the lens through which it perceives events, Adorno's way of thinking is what Jameson claims: a new form of historical and dialectical consciousness. But this answer is virtually a non-answer. Compare this new consciousness with the new consciousness in physics after Einstein. The shift from the Newtonian perspective is continuously enlarging and continuously warranted by the growing density of data supporting it, whereas the new consciousness represented by Marxism is wholly hypostatic and absolutely blind to any evidence that would contradict it. Adorno's vision--typically Marxist--precedes wholly the events it analyzes. As we have seen, it represents an imposition upon these events and is not a discovery from analysis of them.

What could be the cause of Jameson's admiration for this passage and his hyperbolic expression of it in his discussion? Obviously, Jameson can see for himself the criticisms I have noted. Adorno's analysis has no merit whatsoever--judged intrinsically. But it is not, all pretense aside, on the basis of intrinsic quality that Jameson evaluates it. Its virtue consists exclusively in its dialectical character; that is, it purports to find subjective evidence for an objective Marxist principle. The Viennese musician's inner reality is regarded as wholly a product of economic order and thus inessential to explain the cultural expression he gives rise to. This is typical Marxist analysis. As Serge Doubrovsky points out in another connection, "A dialectic that moves from the objective to the objective, turning the subjective into a passing and inessential moment, is a pseudo-dialectics whose phraseology is merely failing to conceal what is in reality a return to a naturalistic causality."[3] Whether Jameson would buy such a determinism were he aware of it is a question only he could answer; but he and Adorno rather nicely illustrate the critical problem that "serving" gives rise to.

In regard to Jameson and Adorno I have made the following general observations which I would now like to pursue in some detail: 1. Marxism's "vision of the world" is wholly hypostatic and blind to any evidence that would contradict it; 2. Marxists do not evaluate on the basis of intrinsic merit, but exclusively on the dialectical character of the work--that is, insofar as the work serves to illustrate on the subjective plane of human experience objective Marxist principles; 3. Marxist analysis represents a form of determinism in literary studies.

Thus an important question we must ask in this chapter is whether it is possible for a Marxist critic to identify any literary phenomenon as aesthetically sound and artistically valuable which undermines or contradicts or works against the Marxist project. The point behind this strategy should be obvious and the answer to the question as foreknown. The value of answering it, however, is multifold: we shall find that on a strictly logical basis any proposition which is not inherently negatable is valueless epistemologically and scientifically (and Marxism's claim to be scientific should not be forgotten); but more importantly, we shall discover through the attempt to answer this question the all-pervasive distortion of human reality Marxist criticism engenders. The Marxist gazes upon the human world and sees Marxist principles unfolding themselves in every phenomenon, and the question I am asking should demonstrate the illusory nature of this face that stares back at him, for it is a product not of analysis of the various components of human reality, but is a product of a pre-existing desire--the accomplishment of the Marxist task of altering the world; a desire which projects the principles of its own existence into the phenomena of the world so that they cannot be missed by the Marxist gazer who would discover them there.

The basis of my criticism of the Marxist approach to literature, then, is not that it would demand of art that it respect aesthetic principles which, after due consideration, it offers as legitimate artistic criteria by which the reader may explicate, interpret, and evaluate a literary text (the attempt to screen the literary work against a theory of literature, or more broadly, against a theory of knowledge, also has a long and venerable history that begins in the age of Plato and Aristotle). Rather the basis of my criticism of Marxist literary theory is precisely that it has no aesthetic, that it can view artistic achievement as only "one of many methods of impressing upon men messages that they could also receive from other sources, perhaps in purer and less adulterated form."[4] Confined to message content, the Marxist's response to a message's worthiness is determined exclusively by its approximation to his political, economic, and social "vision of the world."

The concept of "vision of the world" serves several purposes for the Marxist critical theorist. As an aesthetic idea (and I hope to show later in this discussion that it is finally not an aesthetic idea at all), it is the basis on which the Marxist establishes the unity or coherence of the work. A work has a greater or lesser degree of coherence to the extent that it expresses the emotional and intellectual tendencies, the value assumptions and sense of reality of the social group from which the writer comes. As a critical concept the "vision of the world" represented by the work enables both comprehension and explanation. Thus the concept is a radical exponent in the Marxist's critical vocabulary, for on the one hand it helps establish the identity of the work and on the other it functions as a heuristic device which enables understanding in terms of the social matrix within which it was created and explanation of the work in terms of a "super-context," that is, the historico-political setting, that embraces both the work and its context.[5]

In his discussion of Lucien Goldman, Serge Doubrovsky is especially critical of this concept of "vision of the world."[6] Goldman was a leading Marxist theorist and perhaps the most sophisticated "sociologist" of literature in recent times. His main effort was to blend advanced structuralist thought with basic Marxist critical theory to establish a method he termed "structuralist-genetic." "Even more than Roland Barthes' linguistic or metalogical criticism and Charles Mauron's psychoanalytic criticism, Lucien Goldman's sociological criticism represents the ultimate spearhead of the effort being made by a whole section of the new criticism to construct scientific models of intelligibility for itself."[7]

For Goldman, the signification of a work emerges only when it can be inserted into "significative wholes or totalities." The work itself is regarded as a partial and abstract phenomenon until it is inserted into certain structures derived from its social and cultural contexts. Only then do we reach its concrete essence. In Goldman's methodology, the "valid" meaning of a work is "that which makes it possible to discover its total coherence." As we have seen in chapters one and two of the present work, the psychoanalytic critic finds a work's meaning and the key to its coherence in the unconscious of the author, while the structuralist and post-structuralist find it in the linguistic medium, that is, in the internal freeplay of the work's signifiers. Following traditional Marxist principles, Goldman argues that the work is an abstraction on the level of its internal structures isolated from any life-context and just as the psychoanalyst must insert the work into the personality of the author and his human psyche in order to find meaning, the author must in turn be inserted into the context of his social group if his work is to be comprehended. It is only in this way that we can understand the coherence of a literary work. Coherence is a function of the "vision of the world," that is to say, of the "maximum possible consciousness of the social group."[8] The universe created by the writer is an expression, as I mentioned above, of the emotional and intellectual tendencies, the value assumptions and sense of reality of the social group from which he comes.

The question must inevitably be raised as to why this must be so--why must the writer's universe be an expression of the identity of his social group? Are human aspirations fixed so totally that the imagination is necessarily locked into a stratum of the immediately present community in which the writer lives? One must accept basic Marxist theory here to be satisfied on this question. The structuralist sociology founded by Lukacs, as Doubrovsky points out, conceives of artistic creations as analogues of the essential structures of the social reality within the matrix of which the work was written. The individual of genius, whether he is an artist, a philosopher, a critic, is precisely the one who provides the maximum consciousness of his group's tendencies. This is a general condition which the artist shares. "Although the individual confers a maximum of consciousness upon the group's tendencies, he does not create them: it is the group which evolves them, even though they may exist within it in a chaotic state, and it is therefore the group that is the locus of cultural creation, and particularly of that which produces a vision of the world": "the true subjects of cultural creation are social groups and not isolated individuals."[9] Thus the Marxist must inevitably regard the author as an inessential mediator between the structures of the work and the structures of the group. (We have seen a primitive expression of this principle in the passage by Adorno discussed above.) Thus, Goldman argues, there is a strict homology between the vision of the world expressed in the work and the vision of the world diffused throughout the group.[10]

Doubrovsky's criticism of Goldman's structuralist-genetic is sound but does not go far enough. Essentially, he raises three questions. He argues that literary criticism, as envisioned by Goldman, is a secondary project serving the interests of sociological investigation. Although Doubrovsky does not extend his argument this far, we can see from his view that neither "vision of the world" nor coherence as critical tools serve aesthetic purposes and therefore are not properly literary critical terms but sociological ones.[11]

Secondly, Doubrovsky argues that one can never link a writer's "vision" or "universe" to that of a social group without first acquiring knowledge of each of these separately. But it is inherent in Goldman's method that the two sides of the homologue require each other, that they are self-elucidating and thus constitute a vicious circle which must be broken into from the outside, as it were. However, Doubrovsky does not point out how inevitably the author's "vision of the world" and the "maximum possible consciousness of the social group" take on a specifically Marxist coloring, as though there were no other way to conceive human social relations and individual aspirations. This is how the circle is broken by Goldman--his Marxist sociological principles are self-evident truths that enable him to "see" the homological relationships. Again, the passage by Adorno discussed above illustrates exceptionally clearly how the Marxist imposes his schema of social and artistic relations on the materials he studies rather than letting his analysis be informed by actual facts.

Doubrovsky does object to the _method_ whereby _an_ analysis is imposed, but misses the point at issue in what seems to me the crucial criticism: namely, the Marxist's presuppositions about the structures of social reality whereby whatever he looks upon reflects back to him Marxist "truths." Thirdly, Doubrovsky objects to Goldman's structuralist-genetic assumption regarding intelligibility. If a work's concrete essence can only be known by insertion into the context of the author's social group and that group's identity by insertion into its relations with the total society, at what point do we

stop inserting for greater and greater clarity and
concreteness? Inevitably the critic must expand his analysis
until his project ceases to be literary and becomes
historico-sociological. Again, what Doubrovsky seems to
overlook is the total loss of the work in question and further,
as I find myself insisting, he overlooks how the Marxist
program by which analysis is conducted excludes all other
possibilities entirely.

But most seriously, in the traditional Marxist approach,
of which Goldman's is both a refinement and an elaboration in
light of new critical methodologies, the work ceases to have
any concreteness whatsoever. "[The work's] relations to its
surroundings," argues J. Hillis Miller, in regard to the
Marxist dialectical method,

> radiate outward like concentric circles from
> a stone dropped in water. These circles multiply
> indefinitely until the scholar must give up in
> despair the attempt to make a complete inventory
> of them . . . as he proceeds in his endless quest,
> (the work) . . . gradually fades into the multitude
> of its associations . . . . Instead of being a
> self-sufficent entity, it is only a symptom of
> ideas or images in the culture which generates it.[12]

The extent to which the loss of focus on the literary work
occurs is everywhere visible in Marxist criticism. Consider
the following remarks, revealing in other ways too, of
Jameson's Marxism and Form: "I can well understand," he says
of Marxist dialectices, "that such elaborate conceptual
equipment may seem disproportionate to the daily work of
literary criticism and to the individual texts themselves. This
is, however, to misjudge the role of literary criticism as such
in the process of political education" (Preface). It is only
in Marxist literary criticism that we find such items of

vocabulary as these: postindustrial monopoly capitalism, occultation of the class structure, total mobilization, popular fronts, the international scene, cold war, Spanish Civil War, etc., all of which can be found on a single page in Jameson's Preface.

In an inner-party document, developed in the Institute for the Social Sciences of the Central Committee of the Socialist Unity Party (German Democratic Republic)--a working paper not intended for publication--the author, Elizabeth Simons, makes very clear what is at stake in state direction of the artistic process.[13] The editors of the volume which includes this document offer the paper as an illustration of the serious attempt made by the conferences involved to foster a socialistic literature for the benefit of the people of the socialist states of the world. The essay must be read with a great deal of detachment, for it betrays in every utterance the price paid by writers to rescue for their work some aesthetic value and for themselves a crumb of artistic integrity:

> The continuing development of socialist realism
> in this period took the form of a bitter ideological
> class struggle. It was characterized by contradictory
> attempts at artistic appropriation of new tasks and
> the creative defense of the basic Marxist-Leninist
> positions in aesthetics. The recognition that the
> construction of socialism in the German Democratic
> Republic is a historical necessity and a question
> of vital importance for the nation prevailed only
> slowly and as a result of discussions of principles
> within the working class and by members of the
> artistic intelligentsia.
>
> . . . . . . . . . . . . . . . . . . . . . . . . . . . . . .
>
> After the 20th congress of the C.P.U.S.S.R., there
> were renewed attempts at a revision of the socialist
> direction . . . . Their ideological expression in

> the literary sphere was a serious effort to direct
> Marxist-Leninist aesthetics and literary theory--as
> well as other areas of intellectual life--toward a
> "third way" through the propogation of bourgeois
> conceptions, to nullify their social orientation
> and to separate literary and artistic development,
> conceived as being an unpolitical activity, from
> the planning and guiding influence of the state
> and the party.
>
> . . . . . . . . . . . . . . . . . . . . . . . . .
>
> In the great ideological offensive of the S. U. P.,
> the program for a socialist German literature . . .
> presented a constructive alternative to the revision-
> ist compromises . . . .  In all this a large part
> was played by the discussion on ideological and
> political positions and the interpretation of the
> counter-revolutionary events in Hungary.
>
> . . . . . . . . . . . . . . . . . . . . . . . . .
>
> It is not recognized that the creative task of the
> new literature is to form the new type of German
> worker, the conscious builder of socialism.[14]

Any attempts made by writers to think for themselves were
regarded as "political attacks set forth as aesthetic
principles."

I have given a sufficient quantity of this brow-beating to
establish the tone of these conferences. Marxist literary
analysis serves the purpose of political education and
indoctrination, whether undertaken in the East or the West, and
has no room for individual creative effort. In the inner-party
document, we see from time to time genuinely towering figures
in the intellectual history of Marxist literary criticism, such
figures as Lukacs, Ernst Bloch, and Bertoldt Brecht, rise up
with astute but nevertheless partyline observations, only to be
beaten down by the "democratic" process in genuinely fearful
reaction to intellect.

The object of primary concern for these conferences reported in this paper is "changing the writer's way of life and work" in order to develop an "aesthetic sensitivity and artistic capacity in the working population." This was needed in order to "influence the masses." In every sentence, paragraph, section of this paper what is clear and unmistakeable is that the state wants a power that could subjectively verify Marxist reality and thereby authenticate its statehood. This is the program of Marxist literature and the function of Marxist literary citicism is to serve the state's purposes.

When the non-Marxist critical theorist points out difficulties in his theory and practice, the Marxist critic can only shrug his shoulders and try again. Thus, Stephen G. Nichols, Jr. argues in his article on Georg Lukacs:

> Clearly, the result of the dialectic can only
> be to interpose the critic between the reader
> and the literary object. At every stage, those
> supposedly objective criteria, the historical
> context, the Weltanschaungen and so forth, turn
> out to depend, for their definition, upon the
> critic's own perspective. The circularity of
> interpretation leaves him in a world of subject-
> ive perception, a disconcerting enough situation
> for someone who considers himself a worshipper of
> reality independent of the mind of man,[15]

This criticism is unanswerable. But what Nichols fails to realize is that his own criticism is meaningless in the presence of such beliefs as expressed in the G. D. R. party conferences, where "literary science and criticism began to play a larger role in social life": "it became clear that a meaningful unity between literature and reality, between literature and the life of the people, can only be achieved when the focus of literary efforts is the socialist image of man."[16]

Nichols argues cogently that the Marxist critic imposes himself between the reader and the text; but what the passage just quoted from the inner-party document shows is that what is imposed, in reality, in the body (or should I say in the soul?) of the critic is the image of socialist man. What the critic reads, I have been taking pains to demonstrate, is not a text at all but his own pre-determined theoretical, philosophical assumptions which, through the medium of the text, he will pass on to his own readers. But this is after all his point in critical reading in the first place--his reason for being a critic. The text is a pretext or an instrument to this end: to rediscover over and over Marxist principles.

> Although man retains a modest field of activity,
> he is, as the producer of the intellect, funda-
> mentally "determined" . . . by a "particular
> development of . . . productive forces." The
> formative order of the economic realm takes
> precedence over all intellectual activity of
> man. The ruling center of human destiny lies
> outside his intellect, which helplessly sub-
> ordinates itself to the material causal law
> working from without.[17]

With this essential Marxist vision of the world we come full turn from the ideas of Jacques Derrida discussed in Chapter 2.

There we saw Derrida (perhaps in reaction precisely to his Marxist brethren) arguing that the perception of a "ruling center" in a field outside human consciousness in which man's conceptual structures are grounded and from which it takes its direction in the "play of thought" is an illusion produced by the history of metaphysical thought in our civilization. In that chapter I showed why Derrida's formulation could not work.

The burden I face now is to show why its diametrical opposite in Marxist thought cannot work either. It may seem that there is no middle ground here, that logic compels me to opt for one of these two possibilities. Either man's thought is determined by the material matrix in which it exists and of which it is itself a part or it is not. Fair enough. But the opposition here is not between the determinism of Marxist economics and the absolute denial of a field of "transcendental signifieds" existing independently of man's consciousness. As we saw in Chapter 2, Derrida's attempt to skirt the issue of determinism--as we find it in Marxism--only leads to a determinism of another sort and one that is less defensible philosophically. The opposition is rather between determinism and free-will, or to be more precise, between the idea of human intellect as helplessly ensnared in the products of its own creation and the human intellect as creative of forces which it can direct when it wills.

Marx writes in the _Deutsche Ideologie_ of the development of the ideological reflexes and echoes of material processes in the human mentality: "Consciousness does not determine life; life determines consciousness."[18] Marx and Engels claimed in their explications in this work that the intellect "changes in close correspondence to the economic foundation, concomitantly with the changing relationships in production."[19] This conception, of course, leaves no room for the powers of creative thought, and the poet preeminently is robbed of his muse and degraded to a servant of the economic process. It is precisely in this role that we see the writer in the inner-party document from which I have quoted above.

But more dogmatic is the later and fuller construction Marx gave this idea in the Foreword to his _Critique of Political Economy_:

> In the social production of their lives men
> enter into specific, necessary relationships,

independent of their wills, productive relationships that correspond to a particular stage of
development of their material means of production.
The totality of these productive relationships
forms the economic structure of society, the
real basis upon which a juridical and political
superstructure arises, and to which particular
social forms of consciousness correspond. The
manner of production of material life determines
altogether the social, political, and intellectual
life-process. It is not the consciousness of men
that determines their being, but on the contrary
their social being that determines their consciousness . . . . With a change in the economic basis
the whole enormous superstructure is transformed
with greater or less speed.[20]

The vicious circle in which we saw Goldman trapped is
reproduced here: the homology found between the structures of
the work and the social matrix that Goldman must insert the
work into is a microrepresentation of Marx's deterministic
vision as expressed here. One can criticize these ideas in two
ways: 1. practically, by appeal to the experience of socialist
states and their continuing need to break into the circle by
transforming their people from within into acceptance of
socialist realism as a way of life--a program for which the
socialist hierarchy needs literary artists, as is made
abundantly clear in the inner-party document; and 2.
philosophically, by appeal to the contradictions experientially
and logically that Marxist dogma gives rise to.

The appeal to experience is a critical avenue open to
anyone these days who watches the news on evening television
and who cares enough to evaluate what he sees in the light of
even a minimal sense of social justice. In spite of the
endless conditioning East Bloc countries submit their

populations to, the people there continue to <u>behave</u> as though the material matrix of their modes of production does not "determine altogether" their social, political, and intellectual life-processes. What the situations in Hungary, Czechoslovakia, and Poland demonstrate is that when a change in the economic basis of their society did occur, the whole enormous superstructure did not transform itself into the promised land.

The philosophical appeal to the contradictions of Marxist dogma has been abundant and continuous for several generations now and has never much mattered to the participants in communist ideological debate. This capacity of "believers" to ignore the shortcomings of their belief is the strength of the socialist movement (of all movements, religious and political), and it is not my purpose in this discussion to enter into what can only be an exercise in futility. What I can do, however, is point out self-defeating tactics in critical discussion, where the critic seems to take positions aimed at opposing Marxist assumptions about the nature of literature and the critical act.

For example, Lucian Goldman's major analytical works have been on Racine and Pascal, and Serge Doubrovsky's really excellent criticism of Goldman, to which I referred above, dealt primarily with his works on Racine and Pascal. In his otherwise admirable Introduction to Doubrovsky's book, Edward Wasiolek argues, in defense of Roland Barthes, that to reconstruct the <u>historical</u> Racine in the light of the normative and public meanings of his texts is to reduce them to the fossilizations of the past:

> There is, of course, an objective text in
> the sense of print on a page and objective
> meaning in the normative and public meanings
> of the words. But such a conventional reading
> of the text is a special reading of Racine, one of

> many, and a bad reading at that because it
> is a Racine reduced to the platitudes and
> banalities of the age . . . . To reduce
> the meaning of Racine or Shakespeare to
> such historical reconstruction is to
> reduce them to the fossilizations of
> the past.[21]

This criticism of a way of reading a text is not aimed explicitly at the Marxist critical approach and in its context it serves as a defense of Barthes' structuralism. But it is clear to what critical assumptions such observations are a reaction. The statements seem to imply a specifically non-Marxist critical posture and to constitute an attack on an approach that would regard the words of the text as grounded in a specific social and historical setting from which alone the text's meanings can be apprehended.

The strategy, however, as I have demonstrated in chapter 2, has extreme shortcomings of its own. One cannot disagree with one's opponent where he is right. The objective meanings of a work _are_ the normative and public ones. But does it follow that what is normative and public is therefore platitudinous and banal? Or that to read a reduced text, in terms of one that is read for its normative and public meanings, is a fossile?[22] What kind of license the concept of "freeplay" may lead to is unpredictable and uncontrollable. Derrida can limit it only by appeal to another form of determinism. If one does not regard language as normative and public, one has no basis on which to insist that Marxist readings contradict a work's essence.

It seems to me that psychoanalytical and structuralist and post-structuralist criticism as well as the earlier forms of Anglo-American New Criticism have variously adopted unworkable strategies for criticism at least in part to counter Marxist dogmatism about the meaning and value of literature for

society, Marxism being so much a part of the fabric of critical
studies in this century. However, this is a contention I will
not insist upon.

Nevertheless, with the exception of psychoanalytic
criticism, all the major theoretical movements of the century,
from formalism to post-structuralism, have insisted on the
autonomy of the work of art, in one form or another, either
explicitly or implicitly. And it is on the issue of autonomy
that the Marxist is most dogmatic--as I have amply provided
reasons for--dogmatic to the point, as noted above, where it is
treated as a non-issue. "The art work," says a Marxist critic,
"cannot be seen as a fixed, 'objective,' autonomous whole, but
must be seen in the context of its mediations with the outside
world, as something with an infinite number of 'properties,
qualities and aspects' which are manifested in an infinite
number of concrete contexts."[23]

As a good Marxist, this critic is concerned to show how
social context interacts with a work of art and determines its
identity as a work of art. It would be worthwhile to pursue
his discussion for the light it sheds on the distortions
Marxist presuppositions generate, and for the opportunity it
affords before I close this chapter to advance at least one
"philosophical appeal" to common sense. "A good illustration,"
the author writes, of how the social context determines the
identity of a work,

> is the action taken in immediate post-war Germany
> in banning the film Oliver Twist from public per-
> formance. Such an action did not imply that
> either the film or the book Oliver Twist was
> 'objectively' anti-semitic, but that in the
> particular situation of the immediate post-
> fascist period in Germany the identity such
> a film might assume would have had anti-
> semitic associations which would have been

> undesirable. There was, and is, no suggestion
> that the film of Oliver Twist should be banned
> permanently, or should be seen to be an evil
> film for all time, merely a recognition that
> in a particular situation the identity which
> such a film might assume might be different
> from that which it might assume in a different
> situation.[24]

The author concluded from such examples that the identity of a
work of art is in large part a consequence of its relations
with its context, and that to speak of an "autonomy" for the
work of art is to lose sight of precisely that which helps to
establish this identity: "In other words, we have here a
consistent theoretical basis for arguing that a work of art can
never be discussed ahistorically, in 'purely aesthetic' terms
but must always be discussed in a defined context."[25]

The author's argument here seems reasonable enough, and
the calmness and certainty with which he presents it helps
greatly to make it persuasive. Has he won some ground from us
here, which we must reluctantly admit and adjust ourselves to?
I must emphatically say no! What the writer does not see in
his example is all to the point: far from establishing the
identity of Oliver Twist in that moment of time, the social
context of post-war Germany itself is brought into relief for
us, and the changes in and identity of that social context are
defined by its response to the film. For clearly, what has
changed is not yesterday's artifact, but the society that has
preserved it. The fact that Oliver Twist may at one time have
no anti-semitic implications and at another time may is not
evidence of a changing identity of the work but of a changing
perception of itself on the part of society. Works of art may
fruitfully be used as a means to the study of changing norms
and public meanings in society. But somewhere an objectivity
must exist in order for standards to be perceived against which

change can be recognized and measured as change. If Oliver Twist's identity did change with the changes of society, one would see in the novel or film only a reflection of one's then current social assumptions. It is only because the work does not change that a particular society can see its assumptions as having altered over time from those of an earlier age--for this characteristic, remember, would be generalized and would apply specifically to each human creation of the past.

Let us not call this use of art works, however, "literary criticism." It is sociology. But more is involved here than meets the eye at first. It is precisely Keats' point about the art work in "Ode on a Grecian Urn" that "When old age shall this generation waste / Thou shalt remain, in midst of other woe / Than ours, a friend to man, to whom thou say'st--" not "I am a faithful participant in the changes of your world," but "I am the Timeless and the Untransformed: the Beautiful and the True." In his famous ode, Keats represents the art work as a timeless and untransformed singularity, a created object that marks for man all that is eternal and immortal about him. He sees that it is only against the timeless and singular that the imagination can measure itself. Generations come and generations go in the general waste of time, but the artifact remains--a friend to man.

Yeats takes up this theme as does Wallace Stevens and each spins his greatest poetry from it. It is precisely to that singularity that other times respond in their own characteristic ways. And it is to that singularity of the art work that the non-Marxist critic directs his attention. When one asks the question--"What is there in Oliver Twist that may at one time bear no significant anti-semitic implications and which may at another?"--one is inquiring into the persistent and objective qualities of the work of art. For certainly, there is something in the work responsible for such diversity of response--and it is only by pursuing the work in its ahistoric and purely formal terms that one can find an answer.

For the Marxist critic, the notion of an objective or autonomous aesthetic must be rejected because this view of objectivity is "the cornerstone of a religious world-view, and one which was adopted as its own by the bourgeoisie."[26] The logic here is precisely equivalent to saying, for example, that relativistic physics must be rejected because Maxwell, Clark, Einstein, etc., were religious and bourgeois.

Of all the critical movements and their various postures, Marxism alone makes a claim to our sympathies on ethical grounds--but not because of its theoretical aims and in terms of its processes of valuation. The Marxist insists on a literary meaning grounded in the world, and does not shy from confronting authorial intention, though what it does to intentionality represents a vicious betrayal of all aesthetic principle. But if one is not a Marxist and cannot make himself believe or accept essential Marxist assumptions about historical movement and the human character, both as these are conceived in their interfacing relationships and as they are applied as a critique of contemporary events, then Marxist literary theory and its conclusions must remain suspect. This problem of belief, I am firmly convinced, points up the limitations and failures of Marxist critical doctrine.

Critical theory and the principles which guide it, when these require for their application commitment to a system of beliefs that has as its goal the creation of a specifically conceived Weltanschauung, are inherently exclusive and thus inquisatorial--in the very worst sense of that term. Critical theory must strive for inclusiveness, for if it does not it fails to confront its own character as a discipline; that is, its aims and goals become at one and the same time both less and more than a literary endeavor. In the case of Marxism, if one cannot accept it in its features as an all-embracing philosophy, its critical doctrines are useless for the purposes of literary evaluation and speculation. Criticism, if it is to strive for an inter-subjective assent among the community of

its practitioners must be autonomous and remain independent of
factionalism and service to political causes. Somewhere, such
a discipline must exist--especially in our times when "service
to causes" is fragmenting our capacity to perceive ourselves
holistically in a human dimension. Literary criticism, because
of its subject matter, is the best hope for such a transcendent
vision.

NOTES

[1]Bertrand Russell, A History of Western Philosophy (New York: Simon and Schuster, 1967), p. 784ff.

[2]Frederick Jameson, Marxism and Form: Twentieth-Century Dialectical Theories of Literature (Princeton, New Jersey: Princeton University Press, 1971), pp.7-8.

[3]Peter Demetz, Marx, Engels, and the Poets: Origins of Marxist Literary Criticism (Chicago: University of Chicago Press, 1967), p. 43. The passage quoted is part of an account of Frederick Engels' growing political dogmatism. During his first stay in London, Engels discovered and began to translate Thomas Carlyle for political consumption at home. While Carlyle made his decisions about literature on the basis of theological and moral considerations, Engels's' "derived from an increasingly intense political dogmatism . . . . Literature had long since ceased to be the highest achievement of man. It was only one of many methods of impressing upon men messages that they could also receive from other sources, perhaps in purer and less adulterated form." One might add that in our day there is a vastly increased number of methods for impressing messages upon men.

[4]Serge Doubrovsky, The New Criticism in France, trans. Derek Coltman (Chicago: University of Chicago Press, 1973), p. 214. The problem of causality that Doubrovsky mentions here is

a problem underlying all Marxist critical theory. Doubrovsky goes on to remark that "What may be legitimate for scientific thought, which apprehends man as object, cannot be so for literary criticism, which apprehends man as existence" p. 214. The problem of determinism is clearly illustrated by Adorno's analysis. But I believe Doubrovsky mistates the distinction he is trying to make in the passage just quoted. Literary criticism cannot "apprehend man as existence." This is partly the problem with Marxism, which insists on this thesis. Literary criticism must try to apprehend the literary work as object, but only after experiencing the work. It is the artist's aesthetic task to apprehend man as existence. The literary critic must first enter this apprehension by becoming the work in performance of it. The moment the critic steps back to analyze his experience, he is out of it and it is lost to him. This is why he has no recourse but to consider the literary work as a made object. This condition is the cause of our perception of the work as autonomous. The critic can reflect on his experience of the work, but in order to do this he must apply analytical categories which are his only means of approximating the experience in his reflectivity. What Doubrovsky does not see, however, and what the Adorno passage illustrates, is that these categories (no matter what they are) are always substitutions. The problem for all criticism is that these substitutions are inevitably regarded by the critic as scientific and as more significant, interesting, and telling than the experience itself, which is the only dimension of reality where the work can exist. Who would quarrel with my contention that today literary critics find the experience of the work outside the range of their professional interests?

[5]Thus Jameson, in _Marxism and Form_: "In the realm of literary criticism the sociological approach necessarily juxtaposes the individual work of art with some vaster form of social reality which is seen in one way or another as its

source or ontological ground, its Gestalt field, and of which
the work itself comes to be thought of as a reflection or a
symptom, a characteristic manifestation or a simple by-product,
a coming to consciousness or an imaginary or symbolic
resolution, to mention only a few of the ways in which this
problematic relationship has been conceived" pp. 4-5. I do
not pause in my text to offer an extended criticism of my own
of the concept of "vision of the world," though the concept is
examined sufficiently to leave no doubt how I regard it. It
seems to make a good deal of sense and to offer warranted or
warrantable results to so juxtapose or insert the individual
work of art, until one thinks about it. What is this vision of
the world or vaster form of social reality which is seen as the
ontological ground or source of the work by means of which we
can comprehend and explain it? This is precisely the issue
from which there is no turning. Is it not in the nature of
human thought that one speculates on these matters on the basis
of one's moral, social, political, philosophical, and aesthetic
biases? For example, do the contemporary feminist and
anti-feminist agree as to what the "vaster social reality" of
their time is? And the abortionist and anti-abortionist? The
socialist and capitalist? Arab and Jew? Rural and Urban
inhabitant? To what extent can we rest on an ontological
ground that shifts so dramatically?

6Doubrovsky, pp. 178-218 passim.

7Doubrovsky, p. 180.

8Doubrovsky, p. 181. Goldman argues that comprehension of
the work in terms of the author's vision of the world has no
meaning or is deprived of meaning if it does not lead to a
genetic explanation: "The clarification of a signifying
structure constitutes a process of comprehension, whereas its
insertion into a larger structure is, in relation to the first

structure, a process of explanation. As an example: to
clarify the tragic structure of Pascal's Pensees and Racine's
plays is a process of comprehension; to insert them within the
extremist current of Jansenism as a means of elucidating the
latter's structure is a process of comprehension with respect
to Jansenism but a process of explanation with respect to the
writings of Pascal and Racine" p. 182. Doubrovsky rightly
argues that in the case of a work like the Pensees, where a
relationship between the author's vision and Jansenism can be
demonstrated, Goldman's method is workable; but in the case of
Racine, this relationship is merely assumed and is in fact
forced onto the tragedies. Doubrovsky's criticism, it seems to
me, is really no criticism at all, for it accepts in principle
that Goldman's methodology of insertion is critically valid
where such relationships are apparent. The problem, or rather,
the crucial issue is whether the chain of linked insertions as
Goldman describes can be begun at all. We must find our way
into a vicious circle here. If the principle of coherence in a
creative effort is determined by the material matrix which is
its setting and which, per force, contains structures
homologous to those in the work, then we should expect this to
be true for all creative acts. But in what sense is a
mass-production line or the design of a lathe dependent on
homologous structures in society--of what are they analogues?
We find that the principle of coherence underlying the creation
of the Viking Lander, for example, is determined strictly by
internal purposes, which remain constant regardless of the
vision of the world of its creators. Similarly, one's vision
of the world is irrelevant to the meaning and value of
Einstein's relativity theory. Literary creation is no
exception to this rule. Creativity is an intentional activity,
and, as the differences between Pascal and Racine demonstrate,
authorial intention is the shaping force underlying coherence
in literary work.

[9]Doubrovsky, pp. 182 and 184 respectively.

[10]Doubrovsky, p. 185.

[11]See Doubrovsky, p. 186. "Literary criticism, as envisaged by Lucien Goldman, is inevitably secondary, or at least second in line, to sociological investigation, whose reports it must wait to receive before setting to work itself." Again, although Doubrovsky is right, he misses the point. As I will demonstrate later, the work of literary criticism for the Marxist critic is not to verify its sociological reports but to so construe and interpret literary work as to reflect them. Goldman's contention is that if the works do not reflect a Marxist vision of the world they either lack coherence or are only of secondary importance to criticism.

[12]Quoted in W. K. Wimsatt, "Battering the Object: The Ontological Approach," in Contemporary Criticism, eds. Bradbury and Palmer (London: Edward Arnold, 1970), p. 76.

[13]Elizabeth Simons, "Socialist Realism--Development of the theory in the German Democratic Republic since 1955," in Preserve and Create: Essays in Marxist Literary Criticism, eds. Gaylord C. LeRoy and Ursula Beitz (New York: Humanities Press, 1973).

[14]Simons, pp. 246-269 passim.

[15]Stephen G. Nichols, Jr. "Georg Lukacs: The Problems of Dialectical Criticism," in Criticism: Speculative and Analytical Essays, ed. L. S. Dembo (Madison: University of Wisconsin Press, 1968), p. 86.

[16]Simons, p. 264.

[17]Demetz, pp. 65-66. Demetz describes in some detail Marx's failed efforts at becoming first a poet then a dramatist

and his drift into philosophy and politics. Marx's first love was the literature of ancient Greece, especially that of Homer and Aeschylus. Demetz records Marx's efforts to find room in his growing theories for the occasion of a great literature independent of any economic causation in order to accommodate Homer and Aeschylus. His failure to arrive at a satisfactory explanation of the Greeks resulted in his abandonment of the effort and an intensified insistence on material production as the creative agency of human consciousness.

[18]Demetz, p. 66.

[19]Demetz, p. 69.

[20]Qutoed in Demetz, p. 72.

[21]Doubrovsky, p. 8.

[22]How far can we agree with any of these assumptions? Let us begin by asking whether a private meaning, that is, one that is not public, can ever be known? Or is it in the nature of meaning itself that in order to exist it must be shared and thus become by virtue of the sharing, public? Secondly, do we mean by the word "normative" that which has become "standardized"? This is a problem that besets Marxist thinking. There is a sense in which we can say that the standardized is platitudinous, though this is not always so and the equation must be defended when it is made. But when we say "the objective meanings of a work are the normative and public ones," we are saying something quite different from "standardized and public." Without norms, standards, upon which agreement can be established, civilization itself could not be sustained. Norms are fundamental to all interactions on every level in which they take place and make interactions possible, though these norms do not guarantee success. This is

how standards and standardization differ: the latter, in the
Marxist desire, is an attempt at such a guarentee. Thus,
objective meaning is found in the normative and public meanings
of words. We can go further, however, and assert that unless
the normative and public meanings of language are respected, we
have no basis on which to make sense of anything written or
spoken. So far from being platitudes and banalities, these
meanings are the essences without which language would be
noise. To what extent reading for these meanings may be
considered a reduction, I can only argue that foundations are
what connect edifices to the ground. When foundations crack,
all that is supported by them is reduced, reduced to rubble.
One cannot dodge critical opponents by these maneuvers--they
leave one incapable of thought.

[23]Jeremy Hawthorn, _Identity_ _and_ _Relationship:_ _A_
_Contribution_ _to_ _Marxist_ _Theory_ _of_ _Literary_ _Criticism_ (London:
Lawrence and Wishart, 1973), p. 24.

[24]Hawthorn, pp. 24-25.

[25]Hawthorn, p. 20.

[26]Hawthorn, p. 25.

NATURAL AND CONCEPTUAL DESIGN:
A RADICAL CONFUSION IN CRITICAL THEORY

PART II

# CONCEPTUAL DESIGN

Write, that I may know you.  Style betrays you,
as your eyes do.  We detect at once by it whether
the writer has a firm grasp on his fact or thought . . . .
Great design belongs to a poem, and is better than
any skill of execution,--but how rare!  I find it
in the poems of Wordsworth . . . .  We want design,
and do not forgive the bards if they have only the
art of enamelling.  We want an architect, and they
bring us an upholsterer.

(R. W. Emerson, "Poetry
and Imagination")


## I

The structuralist argues that, "what the human sciences
have done is to chip away at what supposedly belongs to the
thinking subject until any notion of the self that is grounded
thereon becomes problematic."[1]  He argues his case as though
structuralism has absorbed and systematized "the human
sciences":  "The construction of a system of rules with
infinite generative capacity makes the creation of new
sentences a process governed by rules which escape the
subject."[2]  By separating the rules which govern linguistic
behavior from the subject who behaves, the structuralist
dehumanizes and thus <u>naturalizes</u> his field of study.  The
maneuver consists in resorbing the subject into an objective
system in order to dismiss from the realm of inquiry "the fury
and the mire" of human consciousness. : "A whole tradition of
thought," writes Jonathan Culler,

treats man as essentially a thinking being, a
conscious subject who endows objects around him
with meaning.  Indeed, we often think of the
meaning of an expression as what the subject

or speaker "has in mind." But as meaning is
explained in terms of systems of signs--systems
which the subject does not control--the subject
is deprived of his role as source of meaning . . . .
"The goal of the human sciences," says Levi-Strauss,
"is not to constitute man but to dissolve him."
Although they begin by making man an object of
knowledge, these disciplines find, as their work
advances, that the self is dissovled as its various
functions are ascribed to impersonal systems which
operate though it.[3]

The deconstructionist begins with this ground supposedly won by
the structuralist and "deconstructs" the accretions of time and
cultural change that overlay language until he reaches the
"abysm," where language fails altogether and reality and human
consciousness decline into darkness.

The psychoanalytic critic retains the link between
consciousness and language, but for him the human psyche is an
archaic thing which he can probe with a hermeneutic that must,
if it accomplish anything at all, set the subject into a
totality of human behavior in the context of which only he may
render the subject intelligible. "Psychoanalysis--," writes
Serge Doubrovsky, "the knowledge of what in another is hidden
from that other, or of what that other is hiding from
himself--places the critic in the same situation vis-a-vis his
text as the psychoanalyst vis-a-vis his patient. In both
cases, what is involved is rendering the totality of a human
behavior pattern intellegible."[4] Thus the psychoanalytic
critic, though he begins from a frame of reference which regards
human consciousness as an objectivity with its own laws and
topography which can be studied independently and
non-introspectively, concludes by naturalizing the text.
Because the analyst-patient relationship cannot obtain in his
dealings with the text, he must anchor the literary work in the
immutability of a general portrait of the psyche.

The Marxist, by granting preeminence to the forces of history, can comprehend human consciousness only as a product of these forces. He thus locates the meanings of literary texts in social dynamics, since these provide the motivations which govern individual behavior. In the Marxist perspective, man is regarded as the field for the enactment of history. Again, human consciousness is naturalized and objectified such that the subject who acts and thinks does so on grounds which can be inquired into independently of him as subject. "The idea of 'objective' in metaphysical materialism," writes Antonio Gramsci, "would appear to mean objectivity which exists even apart from man; but when one affirms that a reality would exist even if man did not, one is either speaking metaphorically or one is falling into a form of mysticism. We know reality only in relation to man, and since man is historical becoming, knowledge and reality are also a becoming and so is objectivity."[5] As the dualism of consciousness and reality falls away in the concept of the dialectic, all human expression is transformed into the expression of historical becoming.

Why is there a tendency among the thinkers of these three schools of thought to suppress human subjectivity? In literary studies where authorial intention as revealed in the structures of literary works constitutes one of the major evidences for subjectivity and where intentionality itself can be witnessed, these schools of thought constitute major avenues of criticism. On this matter, Serge Doubrovsky reflects:

> From the moment that the comprehension of a certain
> sector of human activity claims to have become em-
> powered to offer an explanation of man, the scientific
> method involved suddenly begins to claim that it has
> achieved the status of a philosophic system . . . .
> Freudianism and above all Marxisxm now followed by
> strueturalism, are all vying with one another at

having one's cake and eating it too . . . .
Though perfectly justified as means of practical
and theoretical investigation in certain areas . . .
which are amenable to positive and empirical enquiry,
they can elevate themselves to the status of philosophy
only by hardening the objectivity necessary to a
scientific method into a philosophy of objectivity.
What they are doing is to use this "partial identity"
of the subject and object of knowledge upon which the
human sciences are based--but which they can never
transcend toward a total identity--and use it in one
direction only, finally resorbing subjectivity into
an objective system and thereby ridding themselves
once and for all of the encumbrance of consciousness . . . .
The philosophy we are being offered, so the theory
goes, is based upon a science, and therefore has the
advantage of being "scientific"; and at the same time,
freed from earthbound origins, can blossom into a
metaphysical synthesis.[6]

I do not contend that psychoanalysis, structuralism and deconstructionism, and Marxism exhaust the possibilities of criticism today. It would be absurd to make such a claim--critics like M. H. Abrams, Harold Bloom, Wayne C. Booth, W. K. Wimsatt, Murray Krieger, and many others of like stature, who owe allegiance to none of these schools, are contributing valuable work to literary studies; and although formalism is largely discredited (primarily by those advocating the new criticism in France), it has become such an ingrained and habitual pedagogical tool that it may well survive and experience a renaissance in the hands of more brilliant practitioners[7]; certainly Jungian analysis has not lain down and died and such figures as Kenneth Burke, Leo Spitzer, Gaston Bachelard, George Poulet, and many others have contributed variously unique and profound meditations that do not fit any of our present-day critical fashions and categories. Similarly, I am not arguing that psychoanalysis, structuralism and deconstructionism, and Marxism have nothing sound and worthwhile to contribute of their own. Quite the contrary, these three schools have vital things to say and are likely to have a lasting impact on the destiny of criticism. However, the direction of this impact tends toward an increasing neglect (for various reasons specific to each school) of the author and of authorial intention, and each school, for its own reasons, has chosen the same means to this end; that is, each views the literary text as a product of forces deriving from some objectifiable systematics beyond the control of individual consciousness.

When we ask why literary experience has been and is likely to remain in some form or another a prominent feature of our cultural existence, these three schools of critical theory must remain silent--just as the physicist remains silent to the metaphysical issues the question Why? gives rise to. He has no means at his disposal to answer the question. But in regard to literature, certainly, the question is not unanswerable and the answer is not difficult but obvious--if we would only let ourselves see it. Psychoanalytics might do better than it does on this issue: The mutual sharing of metaphorical experience lies at the heart of literature and in this sharing we experience the most intimate contact we have with one another. The richer the inward texture of emotion that metaphor allows, the richer our sense of the "good" that is derived from our texts. The need we understand as a reaching out for life in a world larger than that circumscribed by our own experience underlies our motives for reading. Who would deny this? Why would we deny this? What are the consequences of denial and what are the consequences of recognizing and affirming it?

Clearly, the moment we allow such terms to enter our critical vocabulary--terms such as sharing, meaningfulness, experience, and emotion--we confront the problem of authorial intention and the whole range of critical missteps taken in the past to deal with it. Certainly by objectifying the text and removing it from the realm of the subjectivity of the author, we eliminate the problem. However, attempts to neutralize the issue of intentionality by locating it in some realm other than the consciousness of the author must always be involved in logical maneuvers which, on examination, turn out to be unacceptable.

## II

To locate intentionality in linguistic, cultural, or historical forces on the one hand, or in psychic forces to which the individual has no direct access on the other, is to render the literary text a product of nature. Paul De Man, in his much praised and important book, Blindness and Insight, argues for a relationship between authorial intention and work but subverts any gain in the direction I would favor by insisting on this relationship as contingent rather than formative:

> The structural intentionality determines the
> relationship between the components of the
> resulting object in all its parts, but the
> relationship of the particular state of mind
> of the person engaged in the act of structur-
> ization to the structured object is altogether
> contingent. The structure of the chair is
> determined in all its components by the fact
> that it is destined to be sat on, but this
> structure in no way depends on the state of
> mind of the carpenter who is in the process
> of assembling its parts. The case of the
> work of literature is of course more complex,
> yet here also, the intentionality of the act,
> far from illustrating the unity of the poetic
> entity, more definitely establishes this unity.[8]

De Man's maneuver here seems typical to me. The relationship between the carpenter and the "entity" chair is offered as analogous to the relationship between the author and the "entity" literary work. The concept of chair exists independently of the carpenter--it is a cultural item with a pre-existing intentionality which the carpenter "takes up" but does not invent or originate and therefore is constrained by if he would create. Intentionality--the "agent" of structurization--exists in a condition both logically and temporally prior to the carpenter's purpose. In this sense, indeed, the carpenter's purpose is merely contingent.

This conception of an intentionality logically and temporally prior to the consciousness in which it is borne and which is responsible for structurization in the material products of culture is essentially Platonic, though with a difference. The fact that an artifact's structure is determined by the "presence" of its destiny and not, therefore, on its maker's intention locates the Platonic notion of ideal forms not in a superior or perfect reality; the form is not "laid up in Heaven," as it were, but is rather "laid up" in some trans-human cultural system which men participate in and bear, along with their biological selves, during their finite sojourn within its domain.

When we examine this contingency more carefully, however, we realize that there had to be, at some point in history, a coincidence of intention and act, in other words, an origination in consciousness. Once the design (and hence the purpose) of the chair had been formulated and handed down, later carpenters could construct or "assemble" parts into a whole in such a manner as De Man describes. The problem here is one of principle, for our concern has to do with the entry of concepts into language and the cultural domain. Clearly, with works of literature--artifacts which are not exactly parallel with chairs for the purposes of the analogy--one might argue that intention plays as necessary a role in the composition of every work as it plays in the original coincidence of intention and design in the first chair. However, I must insist that the processes of structurization which take place in the making of a sonnet are not analogous to the processes of structurization which take place in the making of a chair. De Man's analogy is very misleading.

Although the carpenter may begin with an intentionality that is already a part of his heritage, it is not on the grounds of this intentionality that he exercises his originality and craft. Shape, color, texture, finish, expense--these constitute the field in which he exercises his own intentions, and it is in relation to these aspects of his "entity" that we are either attracted or not, inspired to buy or not. In the realm where his intentions may be regarded as original there is no contingency involved at all. What I am getting round to here is the idea that the interrelatedness of intention and the processes of structurization obtains in every object that is designed, and that this interrelatedness is not contingent but formative.

De Man would argue, and indeed does argue, that the author is in only a contingent relationship to the intentionality of the work because the synchronic aspect of language as it is currently being defined and discussed among structuralists and deconstructionists is regarded as already a totality and objectified--the subjectivity of the individual being regarded as a function of his language. This is the basic proposition Jacques Lacan's work has been at great pains to establish: the id is "the locus of language's being," an "unconscious symbolic structure, transcendent in relation to man." From these premises structuralists conclude, "man is no longer at the center of himself."[9] Since language is at the center of one's being and is a system of rules "with infinite generative capacity" governed "by rules which escape the subject," the problem of human understanding, of comprehension, becomes also a function of language.

De Man argues, "To understand something is to realize that one had always known it, but, at the same time, to face the mystery of this hidden knowledge."[10] This observation is necessitated by the problem which must emerge from these premises: namely, if the structuring intentionality of a work of literature is regarded as part of or is located within a system of rules and conventions (the cultural forces of language itself), how do we differentiate _my_ relatedness to the work from _yours_? The author's from the reader's? De Man's solution--and this can be said of structuralism generally--is Platonism with a vengeance. Plato was profoundly occupied with the mental processes of abstraction and the relation between word and object that abstraction necessitates. Words, as names for classes of objects, contain potentially the whole natural order, and as to classify things is to name them, the name of a class of things is the soul of that class. Thus to possess language is to possess the whole of the natural order and to have access at the same time to the supersensible order of the ideal. Indeed, implicit in the dialectical method of the dialogues is the assumption that the participants not only can but do come to understand, by the refinement of their opinions guided by Socrates, explicitly what they knew implicitly but didn't know they knew.

De Man is trapped in the same illusion. To say that when one understands something it is to realize that one had always known it is to assume a similar relationship between implicit and explicit forms of knowing--which is an illusion produced by a particular view of the nature of language. It is an absurdity to assume that insofar as what we _know_ is a function of language expression and must be phrased in words, there is a real sense in which if we know the meanings of the words in our language then we know implicitly everything that can be said with them. Plato's argument goes deeper than this--for he regarded language as an instrument of knowledge and not the soul of man. We see this clearly in a passage from the

Republic (a passage which De Man should know, for it bears the
title of his book but in an exquisitely ironic manner):

> Socrates: If so, education is not truly what
> some of its professors say it is. They say
> they are able to put knowledge into a soul
> which hasn't got it--as if they were putting
> sight into blind eyes.
> Glaucon: They do say so.
> Socrates: But our argument points to this: the
> natural power to learn lives in the soul and is
> like an eye which might not be turned from the
> dark to the light without a turning round of
> the whole body. The instrument of knowledge
> has to be turned round and with it the whole
> soul, from the things of becoming to the things
> of being, till the soul be able, by degrees, to
> support the light of true being and can look at
> the brightest. And this, we say, is the good.[11]

Knowledge and the power to learn are conceived as distinctly
different things here. When Socrates speaks of the soul he
conceives of it as a totality of humanness in which there exists
a power with various instrumentalities--one of these being
knowledge--by means of which the soul can contemplate the ideal.
He never confuses language, an instrument of the soul, with the
things of being and becoming. De Man's accounting of
intentionality, however, creates a closed system in which the
reader and the work and language can only be regarded variously
as aspects of one phenomenon--this is the danger of all such
hermeticism.

Edward W. Said neatly summarizes the problem of hermeticism
for the critical enterprise:

> Since the relationship between the work and
> the critic is a self-sealing and self-perpetuating

> one, since the specialized character of the
> relations is exclusive and rigidly systematic,
> a reader can expect only to receive knowledge
> of a sort already confirmed and enclosed by the
> initial definitions. One experiences the text
> making the critic work, and he in turn shows
> the text at work:  the product of these inter-
> changes is simply that they have taken place.
> Critical ingenuity is pretty much confined to
> transposing the work--any work--into an instance
> of the method.[12]

The relationship between the reader (the critic) and the work is
a circular one, De Man argues, with the work enclosed in the
reader's language and the reader enclosed in the work's. "Poetry
is the foreknowledge of criticism" he argues, and the critic
"merely discloses poetry for what it is."[13] Thus the hermeneutic
circle is complete.  In this view there is no room for an
intentionality we may regard as both originating and original.
The locus of value of the work is placed in the circle--it is in
the reader who is in the work which is in the reader who is in
the work, and so on.  The writer's intention can never escape the
confines of the work--and consequently meaningfulness as
conceived in terms of a referentiality beyond the experience in
and of the work itself can never legitimately be addressed as a
critical problem.

"Up to a point," De Man argues, criticising Frye's idea of
art as "aim-taking,"

> the art of taking aim provides a correct model
> for an intentional act . . . . When a hunter
> takes aim at a rabbit, we may presume his
> intention is to eat or to sell the rabbit
> and, in that case, the act of taking aim is
> subordinated to another intention that exists

> beyond the act itself. But when he takes aim
> at an artifical target, his act has no other
> intention than aim-taking for its own sake
> and constitutes a perfectly closed and auton-
> omous structure. The act reflects back upon
> itself and remains circumscribed within the
> range of its own intent.[14]

Let us consider De Man's notion of the 'artificial target" in some detail.

Conceiving artistic activity, as De Man does here, as analogous to the marksman who takes aim at an artificial target places emphasis upon that aspect of intention that is restricted to the act of writing, for the marksman, as De Man observes, is aim-taking for its own sake. This view of the matter locates the value of writing in the processes by which the literary object is created and renders the object's intrinsic interest in the writing, just as it renders the interests of marksmanship in aim-taking. With this in mind, we return to De Man's observation that "poetry is the foreknowledge of criticism" and that the critic "discloses the poem for what it is." What De Man accomplishes by these maneuvers is the exclusion from literary works of all subject matter but that which is the especial province of the critic--critical theory. Other critics as well have announced that the subject matter of postmodern poetry is criticism.[15]

The critic's preoccupation with theory inevitably leads to the scanting of the poem. This helps greatly to explain the contrast between early Anglo-American new critics and our critics today--the contrast between a generation of critical theorists who invested heavily in the poetic productions of their contemporaries and who were themselves poets, and the contemporary critic who produces a three hundred page work in criticism without discussing a single poem, novel, or play. Although the psychoanalytical critic and the Marxist do invest their energies in literary production, their work serves primarily non-literary ends and may be more faithfully regarded from the perspectives of other disciplines.

If we pursue De Man's analogy, however, we must ask whether the marksman takes aim for the sake of aim-taking or for the sake of hitting the target right on. This is not a distinction without a difference, for the act of aim-taking results in pulling the trigger, which is a committment, and insofar as his target is a bull's eye it represents or symbolizes or is a surrogate for something else. In the case of the marksman, his target is an end which closes the circuit and measures the performance. But it is precisely here that the analogy breaks down. The work is more than an end which closes a circuit and measures a performance--the literary work exists in a relationship with readers that has no parallel in the relationship between the act of aim-taking and on-lookers.

To pursue De Man's analogy for my own purposes, I would argue that the work is a surrogate, that it has value proportional to the meaningfulness of its intent and that it is from what the poem symbolizes that its meaningfulness can be discerned. Seen in this light, De Man's statement that the "act [of writing] reflects back upon itself and remains circumscribed within the range of its own intent" would deprive literature from precisely filling this role, because "intent" is deliberately defined as and restricted to the act of writing. To put the case another way, the intrinsic interest and joy of marksmanship lies in the shooting not in the on-looking. If the intrinsic interest, the joy, of the poem consisted in the writing, what motivates the poet to seek publication and what motivates the reader? The reader can never know the writer's experience of writing (though he undoubtedly is intrigued and would like to know and most likely would be disappointed if this uniquely private aspect of creativity could be made available to him), why then does he come to the poem?

But one can of course beat a dead horse. I may be accused here of taking too seriously what was intended casually as a throw-away illustration, and any analogy, no matter how perfect, can be tortured into nonsense by pursuing it. But De Man has taken his analogy from Frye and used it to discredit Frye's point behind it, and my purpose here is to show that De Man's use of it reveals a way of thinking about literature that is unproductive and inimicable to even the possibility of literature. It offers us a view of the critic's mind preoccupied with seeing literary work from the vantage of a critical theory that would render it merely an instance of theory. Other statements made by De Man suggest that I have not been misreading his argument. Indeed, the problem of authorial intention has so far receded from the interest of contemporary critical theory that it is now considered one of the "givens" of critical practice to establish one's theoretical principles which are used to "specify" what may be considered evidence in a literary work. Thus intentionality, if it is not ignored altogether, becomes a property of theoretical approach: "The business of criticism," writes Stanley Fish, is not "to determine a correct way of reading but to determine from which of a number of possible perspectives reading will proceed." And on what basis does one choose a "possible perspective" from which to proceed? Fish answers, "establish by political and persuasive means (they are the same thing) the set of interpretive assumptions from the vantage of which the evidence (and the facts and the intentions and everything else) will hereafter be specificable."[16]

When we begin to ponder the implications of this view, and the situation vis-a-vis the text this perspective provides us, it is hard not to become melancholy--the literary work, as it emerges from the "private, individual, dynamic, and intentionalistic realm of its makers mind," comes into the world virtually unread by the critic. The work and the critic pass each other by, like trains on parallel tracks. Writers write, according to Roland Barthes, in order to present a verbal stimulus to the play of the reader's interpretive ingenuity. Jonathan Culler claims that literary study has already experienced what Barthes called "the death of the author":

but almost simultaneously it discovered the reader,
for in an account of the semiotics of literature
someone like the reader is needed to serve as
center. The reader becomes the name of the place
where the various [semiotic] codes can be located:
a virtual site. Semiotics attempts to make explicit
the implicit knowledge which enables signs to have
meaning, so it needs the reader not as a person but
as a function: the repository of the codes which
account for the intelligibility of the text.[17]

What is happening in semiotics, however, is only one version of
the general tendency I have been describing.

Discussing the reviews of his book, Natural Supernaturalism,
M. H. Abrams argues cogently in defense of his assumption--that
writers write to be understood and that therefore a critical
examination of intentionality is necessary to the critical act.
The resistence to this eminently commonsensical notion is extreme
and forceful and it would be worthwhile to examine a paragraph
from Abrams' essay in which he discusses one of the major sources
of this resistence. Here is the paragraph:

Another and much more crucial indictment
brings into question the validity of the
entire book, for it asserts that the "facts"
on which I rely as evidence are not facts
at all, but my unwarranted interpretations
of the passages I cite. This indictment is
brought by J. Hillis Miller, who . . . wrote
an especially thoughtful and interesting
review of Natural Supernaturalism. Miller
asserts that I commonly "illustrate some
straightforward point with a quotation
which is not 'interpreted,' in the sense
of being teased for multiple meanings or

implications," nor explicated, "in the sense of
unfold, unravel, or unweave." My interpretive
fallacy is the standard one, that a text "has a
single unequivocal meaning 'corresponding' to the
various entities it 'represents.'" But what
Nietzsche and his followers, Derrida and the
other modern "deconstructionists," have demonstrated, is that there is no single or "objective"
interpretation. Miller sums up the basic truths
about interpretation in a series of passages that
he quotes from Nietzsche: "The same text author-
izes innumerable interpretations: there is no
'correct' interpretation." "Ultimately, man finds
in things nothing but what he himself has imported
into them." "In fact interpretation is itself a
means of becoming master of something," by an
exertion of one's will to power. As Miller
summarizes Nietzsche's views, "reading is never
the objective identifying of a sense but the
importation of meaning into a text which has
no meaning 'in itself.'" He concludes, in
considerable understatement, that "from the
point of view of such a theory of interpretation
all of Abrams' readings can be put in question."[18]

Abrams is, of course, quite able to defend his work from the
critical assumptions which underlie this attack upon it, and some
of the points I intend to raise in what follows he makes briefly
himself--but here I shall be elaborating. There are four basic
objections to the views Miller is asserting--views which in my
opinion are in part responsible for the theoretical
naturalization of the text I have been outlining in this section:
     a. If the "text" has no meaning in itself, but has meaning
only as one imports it into the text in the act of reading, why

is this condition _different_ _for_ _Nietzsche's_ _texts_, or Miller's criticism, or more radically, why can't I habitually import into any text a meaning entirely of my own making--for example, my reading of Miller's article ("Tradition and Difference") as a tacit acceptance of and stamp of approval upon _Natural_ _Supernaturalism_? Either one's reading is corrigible to the text or it is not. Miller's reading of _sense_ in Nietzsche is no more warrantable than Abrams' readings of sense in Wordsworth. On this ground, the first and simplest criticism which any schoolboy would make, Miller's position is indefensible and no answer to this objective can be logically sustained--only by ignoring it can Miller proceed to hold to his premises and do critical theory in light of them.

b. If "in fact" interpretation is an exertion of one's will to power in the act of reading, how can we logically deny a similar "will to power" on the part of the _writer_, an attempt by him to import into _his_ _own_ _text_ a meaning? Miller's view implies that the text is a product of forces beyond the control of the author--forces located in the Lacanian _Id_, or in the synchronic aspect of language--and makes a most unviable distinction between author and reader; presumably, only the critical theorist has a will to exercise in these matters. If we as readers exert our will to power by interpreting the text, isn't it logical to assume that ours and the writer's wills meet in the embrace we call reading? Every translator will testify to the reality of this embrace; every metaphor demands it. Why is this position not included among the possibilities? It is, after all, in one form or another, the basis of our understanding of the communicative act.

c. A corollary to the notion that one imports meaning into a text which has no meaning in itself is the notion that writers write in order to present a verbal stimulus to the play of the reader's interpretive ingenuity. It can be demonstrated that the primary historical model of this notion is the poetry of Mallarme and after him the symbolists generally. Valery has provided some critical basis for this way of thinking and helped to extend the view to our conception of the nature of poetry.[19] We have since exploded the idea to embrace first all of literary language and then all language. Critics who espouse it, however, usually resort to Mallarme as their historical evidence and to contemporary writers who espouse the premise themselves in their own writing. The evidence in its very nature is specious. Reasoning that depends for its conclusions upon evidence that predisposes one towards those conclusions is fallacious. The very fact of Abrams' book, Natural Supernaturalism, and the audience of readers who do find in it substance sufficient for conviction and discussion, constitutes persuasive evidence for conclusions in the other direction.

    d. The major difficulty here, however, is the tendency to see writing as existing on the same level as structures in nature. It is true that man finds in things nothing but what he imports into them--the "trepidation of the spheres" for instance--but even if viewed in the Nietzschean terms quoted by Miller, a text has at least as much meaning as its author willed to put there in his desire to achieve mastery over his own materials. To presume a naturalization of the text so complete as to disallow the reader's will to power from embracing the willed intention of the author is to render every literary project impotent, even the critical one. For Miller, it is not a question of Abrams saying "my project is to do such and such, which is only one of the many things a critic can do with a text." For Miller, Abrams' readings are indeed questionable; there is an absolutism in his view which must prevail if one accepts the logic of his premises.

    Speaking of Maurice Blanchot's emphasis on the "act of interpretation," Paul De Man observes: "He frees his consciousness of the insidious presence of inauthentic concerns. In the askesis of depersonalization, he tries to conceive of the literary work, not as if it were a thing, but as an autonomous entity, a 'consciousness without a subject.'"[20] De Man and

Miller, former disciples of Georges Poulet, became Derrideans at about the same time and played a major role in inaugurating structuralist and deconstructionist studies in this country. Thus in the askesis that De Man refers to in his appreciation of Blanchot, the work becomes, if not a thing, as Miller's premises envision it, it becomes an autonomous entity--a "consciousness without a subject." By "inauthentic concerns," De Man means those concerns which derive from the poet's relations with his community. Blanchot, De Man says admiringly, rates explicit forms of insight, that is, insight achieved as a consequence of the intellection and design of the poet, as "inessential matters that serve to make everday life bearable."[21] Instead, Blanchot is concerned with what is present in the work "obliquely," and of which the poet is himself unaware. Thus, though the work is not regarded by Blanchot as a thing, it is nevertheless located in some region stripped of all personality, where the critic can engage the text as though it were a thing. Here is De Man on Blanchot discussing Mallarme--a passage which displays very clearly the naturalization of the text I have been discussing. The passage is worth our attention:

> Later on, in Un Coup de Des, the dissolution of
> the object occurs on such a large scale that the
> entire cosmos is reduced to total indetermination;
> "la neutralite identique du gouffre," an abyss in
> which all things are equal in their utter indif-
> ference to the human mind and will. This time,
> however, the conscious self participates in the
> process to the point of annihilation: "the poet,"
> writes Blanchot, "disappears under the pressure of
> the work, caught in the same movement that prompted
> the disappearance of the reality of nature." Pushed
> to this extreme point, the impersonality of the self
> is such that it seems to lose touch with its initial
> center and to dissolve into nothingness.[22]

What shall we say of a passage like this? That it is typical and representative? An American commentator on a French critic? The voice is carefully neutral, reportorial in tone. There is about it an air of perceptiveness in a scholarly, nearly philosophical sense. It is serious stuff taking itself seriously. But let us pause and consider what it is saying and further consider the interest of its content. There are abstractions aplenty here. Let me pick out some of the more conspicuous of them: dissolution, cosmos, indetermination, abyss, indifference, will, conscious self, process, annihilation, reality, impersonality, nothingness--all of this with great dexterity. Can there be any doubt that we have isolated a verbal apparatus which, just to glance at, is to get the flavor of critical theory today? Many important concepts are here. But we will come back to this point later. For now let us consider what is being said. To this end, I will try to translate the jargon into more common and accessible language, taking care to reduce the passage to an exact equivalence with as little distortion as paraphrase allows--one major transformation, however, will be much to my point, i.e., from passive to active voice: "In Un Coup de Des, Mallarme so dissolves his objects that we see him dissolve the cosmos as well as his own consciousness into nothing." I think this is a fair rendering of what De Man reports Blanchot is saying about Mallarme.

My concern here is not with Mallarme nor with the justice of Blanchot's interpretation nor with the accuracy of De Man's reporting. I am concerned with what is being said in the passage and with what it implies: "so dissolves his objects," or to use the original phrasing with its weight of implication: "the dissolution of the object"--notice how the passive voice suggests that the process is one of more than human action, how it implicates a force greater than Mallarme at work. This implication is further emphasized in De Man's text in the succeeding sentence: "This time, however, the conscious self participates in the process to the point of annihilation." Put like this, the question immediately arises as to whether the critic sees Mallarme doing the dissolving or if he sees another cause of the dissolution, one which Mallarme does not originate.

De Man reports that Blanchot writes: "The poet disappears under the pressure of the work, caught in the same movement that prompted the disappearance of the reality of nature." There is a sense in which this statement must be taken metaphorically. The writer cannot mean literally that the poet disappears, that his disappearance is a consequence of his being "caught" or swept up in some agency of action that transcends him. On the face of it we tend to take such language in a highly figurative sense and so taking it we might construe the writer to be arguing something of this sort: the poet so commits himself to his material that the material seems to take on a life of its own, and when this happens the poet seems to have no will in the matter. Put in these terms, there is nothing surprising or new in the observation. Keats' "negative capability" is an early statement of it, Henry James describes a similar process in the famous "Art of Fiction," and in interviews with authors, especially novelists,[23] the idea that the characters take over the fiction as the writing proceeds is often mentioned. There is nothing mysterious about this "taking over," it is merely the process by which premises lead to conclusions--although the process in other than strictly logical terms may be difficult to comprehend.

The self-abnegation of the author in the interest of the possibilities of his material, i.e., the author's humility in which he gives his material maximum play to work itself out according to its own laws, is a primary cause of the formalists' insistence on the autonomy of the work of art. But in the passage quoted above, there is so great an emphasis on this "movement that prompted the disappearance of the reality of nature," and in which Mallarme is said to "participate," that one gets the distinct impression that Blanchot (or in De Man's understanding of him) is positing not a metaphorical power but an actual one, a movement that leads the poet to an abyss "in which all things are equal in their utter indifference to the human mind and will." Blanchot further notes that as the work is pushed (notice the passive voice again) to its extremes, Mallarme is completely absorbed into it such that he dissolves into nothingness. In the poet of "negative capability" and the novelist who lets his characters "take over" the fiction as the writing proceeds, there is no suggestion that the writer's mind is not ultimately the source of the fiction and poetry, that his will is not in active and dynamic relation to his work. The terms "negative capability" and "take over" are terms describing a stance and their metaphoric or figurative values must be understood if we are to understand what the writer is saying when he uses these terms.

With our stance properly adjusted we should be able to transform the passive voice of De Man's text to the active without doing violence to the ideas represented in it. But if we make the transformation we find that the text is saying something quite other than what it says in the passive voice. If we adjust our perspective such that Mallarme is read as the subject of the verbs dissolve, push, annihilate, reduce--rather than this vague "movement" or "work," we find that the passage is saying some very queer things about Mallarme. We find, that is, that the passage is saying something we might take as mysterious, compelling, if read in the passive voice (where the agent of the action is unnamed and it is implied that whatever the agent is, it is something which Mallarme does not originate); but which we might regard, or more rightly question, as psychically pathological if read with Mallarme as the subject of the verbs. The writer who dissolves his objects and along with this act dissolves his own consciousness could not be said to be writing poetry, and though his work might be interesting from a psychoanalytic point of view, it is improbable it would be so from the point of view of poetics. Again, whether one might legitimately make these claims about Mallarme is not to my point--my point is the critical evaluation and its theoretical basis that the vocabulary in question implies.

In terms of De Man's text quoted above, a further question arises. We may frame the question thus: What are the gains derived by the use of the passive voice in terms of the content of what is being said--why this maneuver? The question arises because of the lopping off of implications, the reduction in mystery, of the passage when put in active voice. If the action of self-dissolution, of self-annihilation, of the dissolution of the reality of nature is seen as nihilistic and self-destructive when regarded as such, as action committed intentionally by a human being, why should our evaluation of this action be different if we conceive of the agent as "the work"? What gain is made by conceiving the work as a process or power or force that subsumes its maker as a part of its becoming? For this is a direct implication of the passage quoted above. By so elevating the work as a power two things seem to me to be gained, both of which represent major problems in contemporary critical discussion.

The first, and easiest to recognize, is the problem of intention. The critic's vocabulary, habitual no doubt, allows him to skirt the issue of intentionality altogether--it never arises. By assuming the ascendency of the work of art in the hierarchy of values to which he is committed, the critic necessarily diminishes the human component of the art, which is precisely that component which endangers his critical assumptions. Intentionality, the underlying authorial motivation which restores the work to the community, must force the critic who takes note of it into his old evaluative and judgmental role. When the art is said to reveal an "utter indifference to the human mind and will," we have come as far as possible to achieving the position of the work as a product of natural forces and simultaneously denuded it of all human meaning but what feeds our critical machinery. The work of art is thus seen as something that uses the artist--who would dispute with a force of nature? It is at one and the same time appointed the highest value and deprived of value. This posture is hard to maintain if we speak of the work as a product of deliberate intention. This leads us to the second gain.

By skirting the issue of intention, the critic is able to regard the work as an active and dynamic force in and of itself. Consider how problematic Blanchot's observations would be if he regarded forthrightly the dissolution of consciousness in Mallarme as a willed effort, a product of intention. By conceiving the work as the active force, the movement, or power, rather than the writer, the critic, by his denial of intentionality, is freed, as we have said, from the burden of judgment. By severing the work from the intellection and design of the poet which lead to insight, he severs himself as well from those insights (perhaps a better word than sever would be insulate). He no longer needs to rely on his own resources as a human being when confronting the text; in the act of depersonalization what remains is critical method and work--the dross is burned off. This is the askesis De man refers to. I do not regard this askesis as an achievement in critical theory; I regard it as an abandonment. The wisdom of Cleanth Brooks comes to mind here: "The principles of Criticism define the area relevant to literary criticism; they do not constitute a method for carrying out the criticism."[24]

### III

Thus the problem emerges of how to achieve a critical discussion of a work in which the very terms of analysis do not absorb their object into a systematics of terms. This can only be accomplished by acquiring a full awareness of the difference between objects that have structure without a structuring intentionality acting as the agent of origination and objects which do reveal such an agent. The lesson that Miller's objections to Abrams and De Man's discussion of Blanchot teaches us is that this distinction is necessary to make if our critical assumptions and the practice which emerges from them are to do justice not only to the artist's work but also to the reality we share with him.

Many things that have structure, thus in a sense design--harmony and balance in the relationship between parts, evolution in form, rhythm, etc.--do not have at the same time a structuring intentionality; such things, for example, as ripples set in motion by a stone dropped in water, the pattern of sand dunes in a desert, a quartz crystal, the structure of craters on the moon, the shape of the solar system (the model of atom and electrons)--all these have properties of structure which may indeed have aesthetic value and may evoke an aesthetic response in an observer. The structures of these objects and events, however, can be regarded as determined by the conjunction of their causal agents in the form of physical laws and random events and their materials.

Thus in each, and in all cases like them, their structures are the product of purely physical forces that are essentially random in character, even though given the proper set of circumstances their structures must be as they are: necessity does not imply intention in the relation of cause and effect. We begin to see emerging here the manner by which psychoanalytical critical theory naturalizes a text. Let me clarify by drawing an analogy between the relation of motive to act in unconscious, compulsive behavior and that of cause and effect.

We know that if we change the conditions that necessitate a certain effect to follow from a certain cause, we alter as a consequence the causative relationship, so that when we introduce event A whether event A' follows or not is unpredictable, undeterminable. In the relationship governing motive and act in compulsive behavior, the character of compulsion functions analogously to that of necessity in the relations of cause and effect. We know from our experience in therapy that we can alter this character of compulsion by helping the patient to understand his motives. But a text is immutable and unresponsive and thus remains, for the psychoanalyst, a product governed by necessity--an object with the kind of structural properties described above. However, by becoming conscious of his motives, the patient can, and occasionally does, regain control over himself, so that his behavior is no longer compulsive--so that act does not follow deterministically from certain conditions which produced the symptomology. It is legitimate to consider the relation between motive and act and compulsion as analogous to the relation between cause and effect and necessity, but with this difference: when we alter the conditions that necessitate a certain effect to follow from a certain cause, what we have done is in effect negative. We have _added_ nothing positive to the situation; whereas in the therapy situation we have added the quality of rational control to the relations that formerly governed motive and act. Ironically, this quality of control we may characterize as a restoration of _will_, and in the conditions of our subjection to physical and biological laws and to cultural conditioning, we recognize this control as being the one area in which we exercise our _freedom_. This will is the region of intentionality in the human psyche and the locus of the origination of all that category of acts which I will designate in what follows as the products of _design_.

However, there are structures that are equally products of necessity and random forces but which nevertheless exhibit some degree of intention. Such structures as the dentition of herbivores and the contrasting dentition of carnivores, the beehive and termite colony, imply purpose, i.e., they are matter organized by some agency for the accomplishment of specific ends which are revealed in the structures themselves:

the mastication of certain kinds of foodstuffs or the perpetuation of the processes reproduction. However, although these cases represent a higher order of structures than the former (I say "higher order" because as structures they reveal in themselves the ends to which and for which they are organized, while the former structures specifically lack this quality), they are nevertheless products of purely physical forces or combinations of forces, their agency of structuration being chemical in nature. But the difference between these categories of structures is useful for delineating an important distinction in what I mean by design.

There is a sense in which the word design can be applied to the shape of a herbivore's teeth, which is what it is for a particular purpose, that cannot be applied to the shape of sand dunes, which is totally lacking in anything to be accomplished by that shape--that is, their shape entirely contains their being. The presence of perceptible purpose in one case and its absence in the other is what has led to so many false starts in metaphysics, such as the design-designer argument or the attribution of elan vital to the processes of evolution. These processes, however, that produce the components of organisms suggest an active property to design that is located in a logically prior, though not temporally prior, condition of wholeness. The problem for us is to distinguish between this condition in its biological manifestations and in its manifestations in still higher orders of structures.

To this end, notice that I said earlier of biologic structures that their "agency" of structurization is chemical in nature. I have chosen this word "agency" carefully because it is an especially useful term for the analysis I am attempting to make. Agency implies means, instrument, which contains the further implication of agent, an "actor" to wield the instrument. In the case of biological structures, however, we are told by contemporary evolutionists that the agency-agent (design-designer) distinction can be fully explained without reference to the supernatural simply by the bonding properties of chemicals in the material. Thus agent and agency in these structures are identical. This is what makes for the common ground of the two categories of structure I have been discussing: the purposeless and the purposeful, sand dunes and teeth.

So far I have pointed out that the one category of structure reveals no intention and that the other reveals a certain limited kind of intention that can be explained in terms of purely physical processes. What this second category noticeably lacks, therefore, in terms of the concept of design which I have been discussing, may best be described as "fore-intention," a rather clumsy word that may seem unnecessary, except that my intention is to descriminate between the word "intention" as used to describe physico-bioligical structurization--or the kind of structural intentionality De Man describes as a transhuman phenomenon--and the meaning of intention for my purposes as the originating power of design. A better word would be "forethought," and by it I mean an intention or set of intentions that exists in relation to the structure of an object very much as mastication of vegetal matter exists in relation to the structure of a herbivore's teeth. In both cases the relation is one of logical priority to the materialization of structure. But the qualitative difference between structures that exhibit forethought and those that exhibit merely biological processes can be discerned in the implications of the word "forethought" (fore-intention). The word implies in its agency aspect a shaping force that is both logically and temporally prior to its materialization in form. In other words, it implies someone who thinks (intends) and something thought about (intended).

Thus we have two distinct kinds of structures: one that is a product of natural forces and which exhibits no forethought acting as a structuring principle; and one that is a product of design, taking the word "design" in the sense which requires the preposition, as in "She has designs upon his fortune," or "His designs against me fill me with dread"; and which exhibit forethought as a defining characterstic. Thus we have design as intention, as a calculus in active, dynamic, shaping relation to some material; and design as structure merely, a passive, static shape that is the property of an interaction between some material and physical, historical, cultural, or psychic forces. To the first category I will give the name Conceptual Design, to the second the name Natural Design. Any structure that is demonstrably a product of interacting forces beyond the reach of the human will is thus a natural structure by definition, and into this category we could place all the immutable structures enumerated by psychoanalysis, Marxism, and structuralism. Literary structures, on the other hand, are demonstrably products of Conceptual Design.

I choose the term Conceptual Design to name this calculus of intention because of the nature of the medium of the literary work. "Sensed objects," writes one aesthetician, "comprise the presented part of the aesthetic object, and may be called a vehicle since they are the bearers of the structure into which they enter."[25] The painter presents a "character made of colored shapes," the musician presents "sounds" with specific qualities, "defined by volume and brightness" and specific durations. In the dance, the object presented is the human body "in motion, which follows a rhythm set by the accompanying sounds of the music," and so on.[26] What the artist shapes or designs in each of these media is a field of sensation, a field to which the literary artist does not have access. The poet's words are abstractions, and even though we must hear them or see them, they do not function by virtue of a design they impose upon sensory awareness. Hence when the post-structuralists argue that the nature of this conceptual awareness is contained in language and has a history of its own that is only coincidentally co-terminous with that of man's, not only is the realm of intentionality that lies at the heart of the poet's work dismissed, but the whole reality which forms the content of his awareness is dismissed along with it. The Derridean would argue that language constitutes the whole of this content--thus every design would be, however regarded by the critic, inescapably a natural design. Similarly, although the Marxist would not regard the contents of human awareness as a product of language, the specific form of consciousness into which these contents are organized would be regarded as a product of historical forces, with the same result. However, it is precisely these two things which the notion of conceptual design readmits to critical discussion: intentionality and the contents of human awareness.

Ralph Freedman discusses a concept similar to my developing notion of Conceptual Design in his essay, "Intentionality and the Literary Object."[27] I find myself in substantial agreement with him, but differ on what I regard as crucial points. Freedman is concerned to find a way to preserve the poet's intentional relationship to the poem while at the same time retaining the literary object as an object distinct from the internal states of both the poet and the reader. "To some extent," Freedman remarks,

> Monroe C. Beardsley and W. K. Wimsatt's "intentional
> fallacy" was surely prompted by their identification
> with an age in which the poet could safely disappear
> to preserve the independence of the poem . . . . In
> getting rid of the poet's self--and getting rid of
> the reader's as well--Beardsley and Wimsatt hoped to
> retain the aesthetic object as an end in itself. But
> if that procedure is found wanting, the opposite is
> equally difficult. If the literary object is elimin-
> ated, if Wimsatt is turned around, and all poetic
> activity is dissolved into mental contexts in which

> poet, reader, and work are merged, we return
> to the eighteenth century paradox and stand to
> lose once more the communality of literature.[28]

The eighteenth century paradox Freedman refers to here is the problem of "How to restore the world beyond the self without losing the immediacy of sense experience as a standard for art."[29] The problem originates in the conflicting world views proposed by the growing stress on empiricism on the one hand, and the neoclassical world view defined in terms of the Age of Reason, on the other.

Freedman recounts a number of attempts to resolve the paradox in aesthetic theory, beginning with Diderot and ending with contemporary critical movements. His discussion of Diderot is interesting, for Diderot's emphasis on the poem as analogous to the gesture language of the deaf and dumb comes close at times to my notion of conceptual design. For Diderot, as Freedman explains, the picture-like gesturing of the deaf and dumb "emerges as a middle ground between the mind's fleeting impressions and the possibility of more permanent forms."[30] Out of this language, Diderot developed his notion of the emblem. "It (the emblem) catches and reflects the poet's meaning; a painting of its denotation, it pulls together multiple perceptions and composes forms immediately accessible at a single glance."[31] For Diderot, this function of the emblem is made possible "by the activity of a perceiving mind through whose consciousness the emblem was formed." Diderot derives his aesthetics from the recognition "that while mental life is multifarious, the mind always acts in a single instant. We see an object like a mountain or a piece of gold, judge it beautiful, and desire its possession in a single instant, yet its description would be drawn-out and complex."[32]

It is from his distinction between a state of mind, which is instantaneous and spatial and a linguistic account of it, which is consecutive and temporal, that Diderot develops his notion of the emblem. The problem with Diderot's notion, however, is that mental experience is not comparable to the instantaneous grasping of multifarious mental activity.

For example, we may in fact see an object like a piece of gold, judge it beautiful and desire its possession in a single instant, but what is taking place in this instant is a complex mixture of emotion, value-judgement, perception, recall of past associations, and desire that, all bundled up, is experienced as a powerful response to a visual stimulus. As mental experience its quality is minimal. We know such experiences primarily as feelings because they arouse so complex a physiological response. We know, also, from introspection that our response to poetry cannot be characterized as an instanteneous grasping of multifarious mental activity, as Diderot's emblem theory required. Diderot had to account for the pictorial quality of language that his emblem theory required by positing a hieroglyphic nature to the syllabic units of language. The notion that gives rise to such obvious false starts in theory is the notion that nature is the subject matter of poetry, and by nature, the eighteenth century thinker meant literally mountains and streams and the flora and fauna set therein.

But there is little in the poetry of the time, or of any time, to convince us that nature is the subject matter of poetry. Indeed, Freedman discusses a typical emblem poem by Sceve in order to account for the origin of Diderot's notions, and in his reading of it shows that what the poem is an emblem of is a complex, passionate feeling, mediated in language by Sceve's adroit use of traditional rhetoric and Petrarchan conceits. We do not grasp the complex design of a poem the way we grasp a scene of mountains and rivers and sky, for language does not appeal to our sensory faculties the way the physical world does. A painting may consist of a sensory design which appeals to our senses in a manner which we say resembels a mountain scene at Yellowstone (yet with crucial differences

which aestheticians still have not puzzled out). But language
appeals to our conceptual faculties and it is only through
some theory that accounts for the conceptual nature of the
designs of poems that we can begin to appreciate the manner in
which we comprehand and the poem inspires.

Yet Diderot's concept of the emblem bears certain of the
traits of conceptual design. The emblatic tradition in English
poetry is basically allegorical in nature. But for Diderot,
the emblem is a pulling together of mental phenomena into a
form which is understood as "a painting" of the denotatum of
the poet's meaning. In this sense, the emblem is conceived as
analogical and its mode of coming to be as the result of "the
activity of a perceiving mind." This emblem is not, however,
available to the reader at a single glance--the notion that got
Diderot into the foolishness of hypothesizing a hieroglyphic
nature to language. The object of the reader is to take the
"consecutive and temporal" account which is the poem and by
filtering it through his experience (and knowledge, and memory,
with all their associational links) to compose it into a
conceptual (not spatial) apprehension which he may refer to,
after the act of apprehension, as an emblem (or design).

This composing of the poem is not an interpretation but
(Diderot was on the right track), based on observation, is an
apprehension, the essential starting point for all further
critical activity. The primary difficulty that beset formalist
theory and which continues to beset it--as well as all other
critical postures for which interpretation is essential--is
that all acts of interpretation, all attempts to say what a
figure means, or what a conceit means; or what a poem means,
involves necessarily the heresy of paraphrase.

Formalists like Cleanth Brooks fully recognized the
inherent contradiction in all attempts to provide commentary on
the poem. They recognized that to interpret a text meant to
paraphrase it, yet they never successfully found a way to
confront the text that did not involve them in interpretation.

Interpreting a poem means assigning a meaning to it; the very act of assigning implies a substitution of something that is in our own minds and is part of our own characters for the poem. The problem that gives rise to what formalists considered illegitimate in such a substitution is the tendency of the interpreter to believe that the two texts are comparable. This idea of the substitutibility of the critic's account of the text for the text itself is the source of all the contradictions and paradoxes of formalist theory, for they regarded such substitutions as a violation on the one hand, and consistently practised the readings of texts on the other.

All such dicta as "the heresy of paraphrase," "the intentional fallacy," "the autonomy of art," "the language of poetry and the language of science," and all such theoretical formulations as "motive/emotion," "intention/extention," "logical structure/local texture," "denotation/connotation," "the concrete matter of the medium/the idea or cognition," etc., are mere strategems to cope with the problem of substitution in interpretation. Thus the formalists were rightly but helplessly at odds with the psychologizing of the psychoanalytic approach to literature, for nowhere was there a more aggressive and unashamedly naked attempt at substitution than among Freudian readers. Indeed, the very method of the psychoanalytic approach to literature was based upon not only their sense of the legitimacy of such substitutions, but on their inability to approach the text in any other way. Human action, real or imagined, spoken or written, is analytically unintelligible until it can be fit into a narrative bearing universal significance.

As Ricoeur observes in his article, "The Question of Proof in Freud's Psychoanalytic Writings":

> To say that someone acted out of jealousy is
> to invoke in the case of his particular action
> a feature which is grasped from the outset as

repeatable and common to an indeterminate variety
of individuals . . . . Such a motive draws its
explanatory value from its power to place a particular action in a meaningful context characterized
from the start by a certain universality of significance . . . . This is all the more true when we are
dealing not with classes of motives, identifiable as
the general features of human experience, but with
fantasies which present organized, stable, and
eminently typical scenes . . . . And taking the
next step, we are ready to understand that
excommunication, on the basis of which an
unconscious ensemble is autonomously structured, tends to produce the stereotyped
incongruities which are the very object of
analytic explanation.[32]

Freud himself considered the relation between the dream account
and the analyst's interpretation of it as comparable to the
translation of one language into another: "The thesis
signifies that one can always substitute for the dream account
another account, with a semantics and a syntax, and that these
two accounts are comparable to one another as two texts."[33]
"'Interpreting' a dream," writes Freud, "implies assigning a
'meaning' to it--that is, replacing it by something which fits
into the chain of our mental acts as a link having a validity
and importance equal to the rest."[34]

Of course, this notion of the replacement of the text by
the interpretation in the mind of the reader as having a
validity equal to the text itself in our experience of it is
what we should recognize as what the formalists objected to in
their assent to the notion of the heresy of paraphrase. "It
was against a background of triumphantly prevalent genetic
studies in various modes, and in an effort to give assistance
in what seemed a badly needed program to rescue poems from the

morass of their origins, that my friend Monroe C. Beardsley and
I published . . . an essay entitled 'The Intentional Fallacy,'"
writes W. K. Wimsatt.[35]

However, when Beardsley and Wimsatt wrote "that the design
or intention of the author is neither available nor desirable as
a standard for judging the success of a work of literary
art,"[36] they meant extra-textual design or intention, that is,
the motives which might underly the selection of a theme and
which might be revealed in biographical or psychoanalytical
studies. The problem, as I see it, of interpretation as a
critical construction which can be substituted for the text
itself, remains a problem, in spite of the formulation of the
intentional fallacy: for Wimsatt explicitly asserts that the
critic's interpretation must always be "subject to the
corroboration of the poem itself. No better evidence, in the
nature of things, can be adduced than the poem itself."[37]

As Ricoeur makes plain in his important book on Freud,
interpretation must be understood as the application of the
hermeneutic by which the reflecting mind must work if it is to
work at all. Thus interpretation per se, is the problematic
that any theory must resolve if it is to be a workable approach
to literature that does not do violence to what it most
reveres. It is only when we understand the problem in this
light that the rebellious concept of the aesthetics of silence
makes any sense, although in the case of those who argue for
such a stance, the act of interpretation is resisted more from
an anti-intellectual bias than from any desire to do justice to
the work. The way out of the impasse is through conceptual
design, where, as I will demonstrate later, the critic can
legitimately claim that his work represents an observation of
the workings of the text rather than an interpretation of it.
This is not a small point--concepts are not concepts until they
exist in the mind as such.

In order to apprehend a conceptual design, essential
cognitive determinations must be made--thus, on the most

elementary level, interpretation may be equated with perceptual processes that make the design of a work available as conceptual content in a certain organization. "The simplest form of thought," writes Brand Blanshard, former Sterling Professor of Philosophy at Yale,

> is, by admission, judgment; and perception in turn is the simplest form of this. The reasons for these propositions are easy to see. First, judgment is thought at its simplest because nothing simpler could yield either truth or falsity. For example, while the judgment A is B, 'snow is white', may be either true or false, this would plainly not hold of either component singly; it would be meaningless to say that 'snow' is true when noting is true _of_ it, or that 'white' is true when it is true _of_ nothing. Hence anything simpler than judgment will fall outside the sphere of thought. But secondly, perception is judgment at its simplest. For with the barest and vaguest apprehension of anything given in sense _as_ anything, perception is already present.[38]

In the case where what is given in sense is _words_, essentially perceptual judgment consists in a judgment of their conceptual content (their meanings)--for certainly the _word_ "tree" bears no sensuous properties of trees. Its meaning therefore arcs across the sensational design of the object _itself_ that permits the _object_ tree to evoke the _word_ "tree" and plunges directly to the conceptual "tree" that forms its unique quantum of content in our awareness. Thus on the level of perception rudimentary interpretation takes place--a fact which must be accounted for in any theoretical model that purports to explain the reading process. It is on this level that apprehension of conceptual design takes place and interpretation plays a fundamental role in the observational processes that precede and lead to apprehension.

Let me illustrate why clarity on this point is essential for genuine progress in critical theory to be made. Any preliminary survey of the critical postures available to the reader will turn up a list of approaches something like the following:

The Ontological approach--which answers questions about the work's mode of existence;

The Epistemological approach--which answers questions about the work's truth in relation to our knowledge;

The Teleogical approach--which answers questions about the function or purpose of the work;

The Archeological approach--which answers questions about the intrinsic characteristics of the work;

The Descriptive approach--which answers questions about the intrinsic characteristics of the work;

The Interpretive approach--which answers questions about the work's relations to the "real" world;

The Performative approach--which involves questions about the critic's identification with the text;

The Normative approach--which answers questions about the work's unity, complexity, originality and seriousness;

The Historical approach--which answers questions about the work's chronology, conventions, economic, social, political, linguistic causes;

The Psychological approach--which is concerned with the work's representation of individual "psyches" (genetic) or the work's power over its readers (affective);

The Archetypical approach--which is concerned with the work's relation to myth and mythical structures implicit in the structures of consciousness;

The Appreciative approach--which is concerned with evaluation and celebration of the work;

The Metacritical approach--which is concerned with how the work reveals implicit or explicit critical assumptions, etc.

Many critics have found it convenient to draw up complex charts with the variety of critical postures distributed across horizontal and vertical axes, with arrows indicating directions of critical interest and flow of critical lines of enquiry.[39] This list is by no means exhaustive, and others may wish to add such categories as the Rhetorical and Linguistic approaches, the Sociological approach, etc. My purpose in presenting this list at such length is to demonstrate not the ideational wealth of the discipline, but the vast potentiality for confusion before ever the work is apprehended as such.

In relation to this array of theoretical categories the practicing critic may adopt one or more of a number of possible attitudes--that is, he could profess to be a monist (which most critics are) and argue that among this diversity his critical preferences are the right ones; or he could be a skeptic, arguing that all critical reasoning is an illusion and that everything is relative. On the other hand he could adopt the attitude that one must cull the intrinsically good, discard the intrinsically bad, and let each critical work have its way if other critics can be persuaded by them. The most extreme attitude, of course, is pluralism--the more voices, the more truth.[40]

Advocating a critical attitude which he calls methodological pluralism,[41] Wayne C. Booth offers an explanatory analogy fashioned by Andrew Paul Ushenko, which I think we would do well to examine in some detail: "Imagine a fixed cone," he asks,

> placed among observers who are not allowed to
> change their angle of vision. One person observes
> from directly below the cone and describes a circle.
> Another observes from directly to one side and sees
> an isosceles triangle. Others at other angles

describe highly irregular shapes. "The
alternative aspects exclude each other as
actual observations--no observer can have
two of them at the same time--but as observable, i.e., in the capacity to appear in
different perspectives, they are connected
and co-exist."

Taken seriously, this analogy presents the
challenge of pluralism . . . each observer of
the cone sees everything there is to be seen
from his position . . . . The analogy pre-
supposes that the account given by every
observer passes at least two of the three
tests that we shall find useful throughout:
(1.) the observations are in themselves
completely accurate; they can be said to
correspond with something that all
unprejudiced observers must grant is
really in the observed object, and they
are thus in one essential respect accurate
and "true"; (2.) the conclusion follows from
the observations, and it is thus valid. The
conclusions are not, however, (3.) fully
adequate to what--as the example is given--
everyone is presumed to know about the cone . . . .
Accuracy and validity are thus standards respected
in every view; in any one mode, propositions will
be properly judged as either true or false, including
conclusions invalidly drawn.[42]

There is so much that is wrong with this conception that it
might in itself require a full essay to delineate. Let me list
some objections:

a. To equate a cone, a physical object in extended space
about which one can gather objectively verifiable data, with a

literary work, which exists as an internal psychic experience about which one can gather only cognitive and emotional reports--barring, of course, such quantifiable data as linguistic usage, dialect, rhyming and such like, those things wherein the work as poem or story decidedly does not exist--is just wrong headed. Literature cannot be reduced to objectifiable data.

b. The cone and the literary work differ in one characteristic that is crucial to the efficacy of the analogy and which reveals the blind spot of all such thinking. The difference is this: the physical object exists independently of human existence--its design, shape, form, or whatever one wants to quantify about it, is what it is by laws of nature. We might say that it is what it is with no _intention_ that it be so. But the work of art is created by a human being, i.e., by a _willing_ being, and has an intentionality that _compels_ us to regard it from certain perspectives and not others. It is a _conceptual_ _design_ not a _natural_ _design_. The presence of this intentionality is what originally gives rise to critical activity and in its absence critical activity would be pointless--analytical activity, of course, could be expended on anything and is not to be confused with the critical enterprise as such. For the purposes of criticism, we must be concerned with intentionality when we are considering a work as a work, for we can regard the poem as a phenomenon (equivalent to a cone) only up to the point where we begin to consider its intentionality. As soon as we take up this question, however, we pass from quantification into the realm of human motivation, will, artistic expression. We cannot escape this line of demarcation, however much we desire to be free from the obligations of our humanity.

c. Booth recognizes that the analogy is simplistic, but not the nature of this difference I have pointed out in b: "Even a cone partially escapes any one perspective; nothing we have said, for example, even touched the immense variation of light and shade that any actual cone will display, and, if I attempt to do justice to that, I shall lose that other perspective I have not yet mentioned, the precise mathematical formula for an 'ideal'cone."[43]   Booth goes on to imagine a pluralist who "would try to accommodate more than one coherent and accurate perspective on the cone while retaining the right to judge their relative adequacy to its inherenct richness." This is the final shape of his analogy. Now I fully understand that he is using the cone as a device to embody his sense of what a methodological pluralist would be like in critical practice.   Nevertheless, "by their metaphors ye shall judge them," as any good critic knows.

What inherent "richness" is there to a literary object, as viewed in Booth's terms, except that richness which multiple views themselves provide?   The richness of the object is contained in the perspectives and is not properly inherent in the object itself.   To speak thus of an inherent richness is to miss the point of the analogy.   To assume an inherent richness in the literary work does not require the extended analogy with the cone and to assume an analogous relationship between the cone as object and the literary work as object is to identify and single out absolutely the wrong qualities of the literary work for critical scrutiny.   With an object extended in space, views from 360 degrees are necessary  to confirm our inferences about those portions of it that lay beyond the range of our perspectives.   There is nothing new in this.   Nevertheless, experience confirms that our inferences have a high probability of truth when based on representative data.   But what data can be considered representative in regard to the poem?   In what sense is it meaningful to talk of "validity" in a critical mode?   "A full critical pluralism would be a kind of 'methodological perspectivism' that credited not only accuracy and validity but some degree of adequacy to at least two critical modes."   I can, for example, derive a great deal of accurate data about the quantifiable elements of the poem--data about time and place of composition, ethnic origins, about the expectations of its readership in regard to conventions of poetry generally and this poem in particular; I can gather data about all things outside the poem to which the poem makes reference and I can gather data from interviews with readers (in the manner of Norman Holland) about how they understood and "felt" about the poem; I can gather data about how the structure of consciousness and the "structuring intentionality" of a cultural force meet in the poem. At no point, it seems to me, can one argue about the accuracy and validity of these data, presuming, of course, all safeguards against error have been observed. Once these data (and any others one cares to add) have been gathered, I am not any closer to apprehending the poem than before I started. What kinds of understanding does such data make possible to me? I can, perhaps, come to some conclusions about the poet's compositional techniques, about his understanding of his audience, about his social views, religious and ethnic background, about the culture in which he was conditioned and his literary antecedents and influences, about the things he knew and didn't know as a citizen and taxpayer; in short, all my knowledge and conclusions are relevant to matters extrinsic to the conceptual design of the poem.

What Booth fails to see is that prior to one's selection of critical modes and the kinds of data they require one to gather, one must have already achieved a reading, for certainly, Booth is not one of those who would regard the poem as a crypt or as a pure phenomenon whose nature is hidden in the vast overlapping workings of reality and which requires detailed analysis to disentangle and reveal and text, in the manner, for instance, of the quantum physicist after his quarks. And this reading is the basis upon which the initial judgment of "work" is made which justifies the strenuous critical labor that Booth advocates. As we see time and again in the journals, this "reading" cannot be taken for granted. One feels triumphant when one achieves it in the classroom.

The question I am concerned with, always, is the nature of this "reading," for it is at this point that one comes most purely and intimately into contact with intentionality--that _being_ or _presence_ which is originative and perceptible as the agent of structuration, the calculus that is in active, dynamic, shaping relationship to the material. Our confidence in this presence is what spurs us to those critical efforts which, paradoxically, obscure it the moment we detach ourselves from it in the critical perspective. Thus the pluralism of critical modes and the variety of attitudes one can hold with regard to them rest upon a foundation which to deny or to ignore is to prevent access to the very thing one hopes to enter via criticism.

For, as I have been arguing, one cannot come to the poem with the notion that its language and the saying of its language are phenomena independent of human will. We encounter poems as the language of _someone_ who speaks or writes and this fact involves us in authorial intentionality. Language guarantees that the author who speaks and the reader who reads belong to the same world, the same culture, the same community. That the author, the poet, is using this relation to create an artistic work complicates this guarantee but does not subvert it or invalidate it. Insofar as his words arc across the sensory avenues of perception directly to their conceptual quanta in his reader's mind, no artistic use of language is inherently, that is, in principle, unintelligible. One does not require interpretive modes in order to construe the work; that is, to provide for intelligibility by insertion of the work into a universal syntax, whether this syntax be psychoanalysis, Marxism, or linguistics. One _does_ require life-experience (including cultural experience) and language experience, and although experience of other works of the same kind may add to the facility of reading, this is not ultimately necessary--for if it were, learning would not be possible.

IV

Although the tradition which has produced the abundance of actual, concrete poems as well as a poetics must be accounted for in any "exegesis," it is nevertheless possible to apprehend the design of a poem by examining its conceptual structures and their interrelationships. One of the most independent and cryptic--and therefore difficult and complex--poets in our tradition is Emily Dickinson, and for this reason I would like to select an especially cryptical and seemingly uninterpretable poem of hers and elicit from it what I regard as its conceptual design. We will need no aids to accomplish this beyond our general awareness and our recognition of her humanity. I will, from time to time, turn to other poems and lines from other poems by the author to help clarify and sharpen our understanding of what we see emerging--but this practice is supplementary and legitimate in every respect, since a conceptual design can be and often is repeated by an author over and over again. The poem I have selected to read is "'Tis Opposites--entice" (J355 in the Variorum edition), and I give it entire here:

> 'Tis Opposites--entice--
> Deformed Men--ponder Grace--
> Bright fires--the blanketless--
> The Lost--Day's face--
>
> The Blind--esteem it be
> Enough Estate--to see--
> The Captive--strangles new--
> For deeming--Beggars--play
>
> To lack--enamor Thee--
> Tho' the Divinity--
> Be only
> Me

The identification of the speaking voice with the "Divinity" and its use of the imperative in the phrase "enamor Thee" create an opposition the meaning of which seems almost too private to construe. But once the conceptual design of the poem begins to emerge, I think we will see these terms with an exceptional clarity. We will see that the design of the poem represents a doctrine in which its method of composition in the broadest sense becomes identical with its meaning, and acquires both spiritual and aesthetic value.

The opening line--"'Tis Opposites--entice"--states a principle, a mechanical one if you will, taken from the common lore of physics. The mechanism of enticement suggested by the line is that of the opposition of magnetic poles, where attraction is motivated by a positive in relation to a negative. This concept underlies the whole poem and initiates the controlling idea that is devleoped into a doctrine of poetic method. The three sets of terms which follow this line serve to illustrate the physical character of opposition and enticement and at the same time serve to remove the realm of the poem's meaning from the physical world. There thus begins to emerge a dialetic which itself reflects the "enticing" opposition stated in the first line. For just as on the physical level the mechanism of enticement is a positive in relation to a negative pole, so on a spiritual or meta-physical level the mechanism of enticement is a perception of value (positive) in relation to the perceiver's condition or lack (negative) of that value. This, I think, is clear from the nature of the three sets of terms in the first stanza, each of which admits both a physical and spiritual meaning (the method of poetic creation suggested by the poem as a whole).

The three sets of terms in the first stanza are grace and deformed men, fire and the blanketless, day and the lost. On the physical plane grace, of course, is conceived as the opposite of deformity, or beauty of form and proportion; fire in the sense of the element, the source of heat and vitality;

day in the sense of light, vision, purpose, direction, etc. On the spiritual or metaphysical plane, however, grace is conceived in the sense of wholeness, propriety, sanctity; fire in its usual symbolic meaning of passion; day as understanding, intuitive apprehension. Together, these elements on both levels form the fullness or perfection of human consciousness. That my attribution of such conceptual content to these terms is not arbitrary is suggested by the fact that in each set of terms there is a conscious mind in a negative relation to the positive value: denied grace by his deformity, the deformed man ponders grace; and each of the following sets is coordinated upon the verb "ponder." Thus the mechanism of attraction acquires, by virtue of the terms used to express it, both a physical and spiritual value, the one standing in analogical relationship to the other, and the realm of meaning of the design is thus shifted to the upward plane of the developing conception of the poem.

This is an incredible compression of meaning, one of the real triumphs of Dickinson's conceptual design here, which, as has been shown, is itself the meaning of the developing context; meaning and method are so interpenetrating here as to be simultaneous and indivisible. One finds much evidence in her poetry of this contrast or opposition between the physical and the spiritual, positive value and "being" in a state of lack. One recalls at random: "To comprehend a nectar / requires sorest need," "much Madness is divinest Sense," "I taste a liquor never brewed," "To learn the Transport by the Pain / As Blind Men learn the sun!", etc. There is about the borders of the conception the suggestion that the imaginative effort to achieve the value is simultaneously to create it in its aesthetic dimensions and to enhance the condition of lack. The quality of emotion such a condition would engender accounts for the strangeness and queerness of emotion permeating that most mysterious of her poems "Further in summer than the Birds."

To return to the poem above, however, the context so far suggests a twofold conception. It suggests first a cleavage between value and reality, between the metaphysical and physical; a cleavage that is perhaps bridged naturally by the attainment of grace, passion, and understanding. Secondly, it suggests that when the condition of the perceiving mind is deprived of the capacity to achieve these values, their lack becomes the motive of enticement which transforms experience into art. This second conception is, since it depends upon the first and is an extension of its implications, what the poem is ultimately resolving itself to express. The second and third stanzas are extremely cryptic and at first seem to resist any penetration at all. Their resolution into the design depends upon the reader realizing that the poem is one part of a dialogue, a response in the voice of the author's persona to a question or questions put by the author. The perception of this distinction is what organizes the elements of the next two stanzas and is implicit in the first; but we can find it as an organizing principle at work in earlier poems by Dickinson. The distinction, however, between persona and poet, it need hardly be pointed out, continues and is, as will be seen later, the point of the earlier distinction between the metaphysical and physical, value and lack, that I have been discussing. The persona represents, as it is the speaking voice, that part of consciousness which has created the poem in response to the poet's "sorest need," and represents further that perfection of the consciousness which naturally bridges the gap between the metaphysical and physical, value and being. It is only in this sense that its reference to itself as "the Divinity" may be understood.

If the first stanza illustrates the physics and metaphysics of poetic perception, the second illustrates the aesthetic rationale of creation. This seems clear just from a comparison of the verbs: entice and ponder in the first stanza; esteem and deem in the second, with the curious image between them of the captive strangling new (which suggests the rationale of the dense cryptological form of her design). Here, _esteem_ conveys an element of appreciation and _deem_ an element of judgment, each an extension of the meanings implied in the ponder of the first stanza, thus creating a continuously expanding context which binds the two stanzas together. Unless we read the verbs as a developing continuum of meaning, the two stanzas would seem to lose their formal interdependency, since the three sets of terms in the second stanza do not reflect the clearly bi-polar oppositions developed in the sets of the first stanza; and the terms would seem not to reflect the positive/negative attributes of the sets in the first which shift the context of meaning upward into the poem's metaphysical implications. It is unnecessary to argue that the perception of formal unity in Dickinson's poems depends upon the ingenuity of a sympathetic reader--though some may rightly argue that the effort is itself the reader's obligation to the poem, and that usually the unity is there to be found and is not illusory (this also is part of her meaning)--nevertheless, the poet does cast her poem unaided and irrevocably into its realm of meaning. The continuum, however, suggested by the verbs ponder, esteem, deem do lead into bi-polar oppositions with a positive/negative value to the terms. The realm of meaning has expanded, and the focus has shifted, and in the context of aesthetic doctrine now being illustrated one must expect to find the formal relationships on a different level.

Rather than within sets, the oppositions now obtain between sets of terms. With the model of magnetic poles before him, the reader can relate the Blind who esteem it enough to see and the Beggars who deem in order to play to the aesthetic rationale of creation. The former, in the act of esteeming, "see," they create the aesthetic context; the latter deem or judge by "playing" amid the structure thus created. These are beggars because they come to the aesthetic object in the posture of lack, lack of what the object offers: _insight_, grace, passion; in short, the fullness of life. The former are blind because it is their estate, as with Tiresias, to see with fullness and clarity: they "know" the transport by the pain. These then are the magnetic poles, the one positive, the other negative, which now serve to illustrate the aesthetic dimension of poetic activity. The current between the poles "captures" the poem's meaning and structures it or patterns it as a real magnetic force structures the metal filings that are "caught" in its grip. The captive thus strangles new whenever a reader--beggar--comes to the poem, for he is himself the negative pole which completes the "circuit," so to speak.

The two stanzas thus appear to be almost magically interdependent and interpenetrating: it has been shown how the first stanza set up the relations between the physics and metaphysics of poetic perception, and how the method and meaning merge into a single and simultaneous act; as with ripples radiating from a point, meaning expands from method to larger method, from perception to conception, as it were, with the process itself becoming the meaning or rationale of the act in the second stanza. Thus the first stanza relates to the second as the physics of creation relate to the metaphysics. The poem expands also from its creator to embrace and circumscribe the relation between creator and reader, extending the polar oppositions to their ultimate degree.

It is time to consider the third and most cryptic stanza. Again, there appears to be a breakdown, a loss of continuity between the context as it has been followed so far and the final statement of the poem. There is most notably a shift of focus here, with a direction taken that seems hardly to relate to what has come before. The speaking voice identifies itself, and refers to itself as "the Divinity." Further, it asks the reader, apparently, to enamor himself. It refers to a lack but does not specify. This is all inexplicable and appears to break down completely in Dickinson's urge to keep private meaning locked in the crypt of the poem. However, as I suggested above, "'Tis Opposites--entice" is essentially a response of the persona to the poet, which establishes two distinct points of view.

The poet and persona, then, are separate identities, the meanings of which share the physical/metaphysical values outlined in the above discussion. The two poems I would like to discuss briefly before returning to the last stanza treat of this distinction and clearly evaluate and assign symbolic meaning to the terms thus set up in "opposition." The first is "You see I cannot see--your Lifetime" (J253). Here is the poem entire:

> You see I cannot see--your Lifetime--
> I must guess--
> How many times it ache for me--today--Confess--
> How many times for my far sake
> The brave eyes film--
> But I guess guessing hurts--
> Mine--get so dim!
>
> Too vague--the face--
> My own--so patient--covers--
> Too far--the strength--
> My timidness enfolds--
> Haunting the Heart--
> Like her translated faces--
> Teazing the want--
> It--only--can suffice!

Here a person is addressed directly. From the first line the I-you relationship is intimate and involved in some sorrow, which the first stanza attempts to confess. The eyes of the person addressed film; the eyes of the speaker get dim. There is clearly a mutual involvement suggested, with the speaker unable to ascertain what it wants to know about the other. At

the conclusion of the first stanza the I-you form of direct
address ends.  The second stanza begins as a meditation on the
part of the speaker, with a shift in the manner of address,
where, as usual in meditative poems, the person addressed is a
general you or even the self.  The you of the first stanza
appears here in the third person as "the face," "the strength,"
and as the referent of the pronoun "her."  That the I-you in
the poem refers to the poet-persona distinction seems clear
from the manner of phrasing of the first four lines of the
second stanza:  as one reads them carefully, one notices an
inversion of the subject-object in the two, paired, parallel
constructions.    In    the    first,    "the    face--/My    own--so
patient--covers," either "my own" or "the face" is doing the
covering.  Of course, this merging of faces suggests that
either way the identity is the same, since the poet-persona
distinction is meant to characterize two aspects of the self.
The second construction is exactly similar in its controlled
ambiguity.  The speaker's heart is haunted, teased by the
"want" (a lack), which is want of the original of the
"translated faces."  The object of the want, the "It" of the
final line, is all that can suffice, the fulfillment of desire
of the speaking voice.  This voice is the voice of the poet,
which can only translate the voice of the persona (the
metaphysical self), and the poems which are the result--the
translated faces--are haunted by the presence in them of the
persona, though in a changed, albeit physical condition.

One can see clearly how Dickinson evaluates the two
aspects of the creative mind, which is what these poems are
about, by comparing the symbolic values of the Jewel and the
Amethyst in "I held a Jewel in my fingers" (J245).  Here is the
poem:

> I held a Jewel in my fingers--
> And went to sleep--
> The day was warm, and winds were prosy--
> I said "'Twill keep--

> I woke--and chid my honest fingers,
> The Gem was gone--
> And now, an Amethyst remembrance
> Is all I own--

Here, in the warm and prosy air, she holds a Jewel and goes to sleep. When she wakes, it is gone and all she has is an "Amethyst remembrance." An amethyst, it should be noted, is a kind of quartz purple to violet in color which is used as a gemstone, or imitation gem. In the relationships patterned by this distinction, both the color and substance are of important symbolic value. The Jewel is associated with day, the Amethyst with dim imitation of common material. It must also be pointed out that amethyst is a word used to denote an anti-intoxicant, or a remedy for intoxication, stemming from the Greek. These associations clearly assign to the persona-poet distinction the values of what may today be described as epiphanic and normal consciousness. By association the Jewel is the metaphysically rich, all that the Amethyst lacks, but symbolizes. The Jewel-Persona, Amethyst-Poet association clearly assigns values to the states of mind each of them represent, values which enable us to comprehend the quality of emotion expressed by the first of these two poems.

Since the order of composition of these three poems is the reverse of the order in which I discussed them, there may be some justification in turning to these earlier poems in order to clarify a distinction which they have in common. One is at least in a better position to understand more sympathetically the reference of the speaking voice to herself as "the Divinity" in "'Tis Opposites--entice." The association of the Jewel with day, with the precious in the context of the "prosy," and with intoxication (epiphany), together with its ordinary associations with beauty, focuses the three sets of terms in the first stanza of "'Tis Opposites--entice" into a single image for us. This enables one to grasp the relevance

of a curious feature in this stanza: the structural inversion
of the middle set of terms with respect to the other two. One
notices that the subject here takes the position of the object
in the other two sets. This set refers to fire and the
blanketless. One finds that the word "enamor"--to inflame with
love--in the third stanza thus seems to be answering to a
question or desire suggested by the structural pattern of the
first stanza. So there arises from the design an intimation of
what it is that the poet lacks, the fire, passion, epiphany
symbolized in the contrast between the Jewel and the Amethyst.
These are the especial province of the persona, that which only
can suffice, as suggested in the earlier poem. The opposition,
then, between the "Thee" and the "Me" of the third stanza
enlarges the growing context of the poem to its final and
logical resting place: the transformation into art of the
poet's experience in order to satisfy the yearning for fullness
and completeness, a state of "being" symbolized by the persona,
which is denied her by virtue of her "prosy" physical
existence.

It would seem, then, that the concepts of "'Tis
Opposites--entice" are multileveled and complex, making a far
more complex design than either of the two earlier poems. It
is conceived as a dialectic of opposites, where values assigned
to the paired terms move the procession of meaning into larger
dialectical frameworks, ultimately arriving at an estimation of
the poet's normal life and that "Divine" characteristic which
unifies experience into conceptual or meaningful wholes. The
attraction between the two poles results in the poem, which, it
is further suggested, becomes one part of the dialectic between
artifact and contemplator, the ultimate rationale, or purpose
as it were, of the internal oppositions between the poet and
her persona.

What we discover from eliciting the multifold conceptual
phenomena of this poem is that before any critical work can
begin we must understand how these phenomena are ordered and

organized in the poetic experience, how they interrelate in the context of the overall design, which is what masters them and renders them obedient to the author's intention. Our acts of interpretation of the individual concepts are perceptions of the elements of design and our conception of the whole is a "pre-understanding" of the text--that is, it constitutes the basis upon which critical activity can then take place.

This pre-understanding is the necessary initial movement toward the text and is guided by the desire to understand and is motivated by the basic questions one brings to any human expression.[44] "We need to recover the relation between the work and truth," Michael Murray argues in his phenomenological approach to the "Critical Present":

> If we liberate the concept of style from
> its usual structures as decoration, fashion,
> or embellishment, and from the notion of it
> as merely a medium or a predicate of some
> deeper substratum of articulation, then we
> are on the threshold of an authentic concep-
> tion of literature.[45]

I think that we have demonstrated how, in Dickinson's poem, meaning arises not from some "deeper substratum of articulation" beyond the design of the poet, as something "predicated" by an unnameable "force"; but rather from an observable intentionality which we discover as inherent in the conceptual design of the poem.

NOTES

[1]Jonathan Culler, Structuralist Poetics: Structuralism, Linguistics, and the Study of Literature (Ithaca, New York: Cornell University Press, 1975), pp. 28-29.

[2]Culler, p. 29. Culler argues both ways with regard to the question raised here. Although "thought thinks, speech speaks and writing writes," Culler explains, "Individuals choose when to speak and what to say," etc. But these acts "are made possible by a series of systems which the subject does not control." Structuralist research in the areas of linguistics, psychoanalysis, sociology, anthropology have "decentered" the subject in relation to "laws of its desire, the forms of its language, the rules of its action, or the play of its mythical and imaginative discourse" (p. 29).

[3]Culler, Pursuit of Signs (Ithaca, New York: Cornell University Press, 1981), p. 33.

[4]Serge Doubrovsky, The New Criticism in France, trans. Derek Coltman (Chicago: The University of Chicago Press, 1973), p. 241.

[5]From Antonio Gramsci, Selections from the Prison Notebooks of Antonio Gramsci, quoted in Jeremy Hawthorn, Identity and Relationship: A Contribution to Marxist Theory of Literary Criticism (London: Lawrence & Wishart, 1973), p. 19.

[6]Doubrovsky, p. 225.

[7]See my discussion with Cleanth Brooks, "Sounding the Past: A Discussion with Cleanth Brooks," in The Missouri Review, Fall (1982), for some interesting comments by Brooks on the pedagogical value of contemporary critical approaches.

[8]Paul De Man, "Form and Intent in The American New Criticism," in Blindness and Insight: Essays in the Rhetoric of Contemporary Criticism (New York: Oxford University Press, 1971), p. 25.

[9]For an excellent criticism of Lacanian psychoanalysis, see Doubrovsky's discussion, pp. 311-13. Doubrovsky concludes his discussion with the harsh judgment that the Lacan school is a theoretical travesty which itself cries out for psychoanalysis. He bases his criticism essentially on the notion I have raised here: "any interpretation that ousts the subject from centrality in favor of some kind of material or formal 'laws,' is simply in error and a betrayal of experience itself, which is the sole basis upon which science is possible." The ousting of the subject is a necessary concomitant of the naturalization of the human psyche and is not, I feel, a proof of the nihilism Doubrovsky sees it as.

[10]De Man, "Form and Intent," p. 32.

[11]See Plato, Republic (VII, 518), in Greek Philosophy: Thales to Aristotle, ed. Reginald E. Allen (New York: The Free Press, 1966), p. 201.

[12]Edward W. Said, "Roads Taken and Not Taken," in Directions for Criticism: Structuralism and its Alternatives, eds. Murray Krieger and R. S. Dembo (Madison, Wisconsin: The University of Wisconsin Press, 1977), pp. 39-40.

[13]De Man, "Form and Intent," p. 31.

[14]De Man, "Form and Intent," p. 26. As a criticism of Frye's formalism and restricted sense of intention, De Man's argument out-Fryes Frye. There is little difference between their views, it seems to me, except the vocabulary in which they are expressed.

[15]See the comments on this problem in Robert Boyers, R. P. Blackmur: Poet-Critic--Toward a View of Poetic Objects (Columbia, Missouri: University of Missouri Press, 1980), p. 3.

[16]See William E. Cain's discussion of Fish's position (which also quotes this passage) in "Directions for Criticism: Geoffrey Hartman and Stanley Fish," The Missouri Review, Summer (1981), pp. 117-29.

[17]The essay is part of a dialogue in Wayne C. Booth, Critical Understanding: The Powers and Limits of Pluralism (Chicago: University of Chicago Press, 1979), p. 186. For the review by Miller, see Diacritics, 2 (1972), 11-12.

[18]See Gerald Bruns, Modern Poetry and The Idea of Language: A Critical and Historical Study (New Haven: Yale University Press, 1974). Bruns argues that we derive from Valery the notion that poetry and practical uses of language differ essentially in the degree to which language deflects meaning: in the practical use of language, form does not outlive meaning; in the poetic, form deflects meaning in order to resonate in the foreground of our awareness. In essence, I do not argue with this notion, except that I would add to it the caution that this deflection of meaning for the purposes of foregrounding should not be regarded as itself the meaning and value of the poetic object--which is the heart of the issue.

[19]De Man, "Impersonality in the Criticism of Maurice Blanchot," in Blindness and Insight, p. 78.

[20]De Man, "Impersonality," p. 78.

[21]De Man, "Impersonality," pp. 72-73.

[22]See the interviews with fiction writers--especially with Saul Bellow--in The Contemporary Writer, Interviews with Sixteen Novelists and Poets, ed. L. S. Dembo (Madison, Wisconsin Press, 1972).

[23]For an excellent discussion of Brooks' "Formalist Credo," see the essay by Kenneth Burke, "Formalist Criticism: Its Principles and Limits," in Language As Symbolic Action (Berkeley: University of California Press, 1966), pp. 485-490.

[24]Arthur Berndtson, Art, Expression, and Beauty (Chicago: Holt, Rinehart and Winston, Inc., 1969), p. 25.

[25]Berndtson, pp. 24-28.

[26]Ralph Freedman, "Intentionality and the Literary Object," in Krieger and Dembo, Directions for Criticism, pp. 137-160.

[27]Freedman, pp. 149-150.

[28]Freedman, p. 143.

[29]Freedman, p. 144.

[30]Freedman, p. 144.

[31]Paul Ricoeur, "The Question of Proof in Freud's Psychoanalytic Writings," Journal of American Psychoanalytic Association, 25:4 (1977), p. 864.

[32] Paul Ricoeur, _Freud and Philosophy: An Essay on Interpretation_ (New Haven: Yale University Press, 1970), p. 89.

[33] Quoted in Ricoeur, _Freud and Philosophy_, p. 89.

[34] W. K. Wimsatt, "Genesis: A Fallacy Revisited," in _Issues in Contemporary Literary Criticism_, ed. Gregory T. Polletta (Boston: Little, Brown and Company, 1973), p. 256.

[35] Wimsatt, p. 274.

[36] Wimsatt, p. 274.

[37] Brand Blanshard, _The Nature of Thought_ vol. I (London: George Allen and Unwin Ltd., 1939), pp. 51-52. "Perception is not perception," writes Blanshard, "unless it supplies us a ground in sensation for something that goes beyond this. But if sensation is present alone, we are below the perceptual level; judgment, or something like judgment, must be present also. If, for example, when we looked at the dress we were aware of nothing but blue, we should not in strictness be perceiving; perceiving proper could appear when we took the blue _as_ something--as the colour of the dress, or as one of the series of colours, or even merely as blue. Sensation is the nether limit of perception. Explicit judgment is the upper limit. We are clearly beyond mere perceiving when judgment is made reflectively, when what we assert is no longer taken as simply presented, but is recognized as a venture of our own that may be mistaken. For example, if the light raised doubts about the colour and we said 'That is a darker blue than it looks', we should have passed beyond mere perception into the region of explicit judgment" (pp. 53-54). Similarly, when we comprehend the intention of _irony_, for example, in a phrase, we are beyond the level of perception of its conceptual content and involved in a higher order of interpretation. But the

conceptual content of the words must be judged as such in the perception of them as words or no comprehension at all has taken place.

[38]I have taken most of this list from Richard Macksey, ed., Velocities of Change: Critical Essays from M.L.N. (Baltimore: The Johns Hopkins University Press, 1974), pp. XXII-XXIV. Macksey argues that there would be less critical disagreement if critics only faced up to the metacritical task of discriminating which critical languages they invoked as well as which critical questions they asked. But I don't believe critics are generally confused over these matters. The confusion arises from deeper sources which have to do with the orientation of the critic towards fundamental questions concerning the nature of man and his consciousness.

[39]See Wayne C. Booth, pp. 8-24, for a full discussion of these attitudes, which I have abbreviated in number here for the sake of management.

[40]From this perspective, Booth argues, critics can recognize that their conflicting critical positions may be entirely acceptable on the basis of a "higher semantics," by which they can discover the differing "worlds of discourse" implied by their irreconcilable views. The virtue of this position is its seeming common sense, but when we realize that the phrase "higher semantics" is really a euphemism for "transcendence," it becomes difficult to accept. Mankind has never achieved such a perspective: in the Falkland Islands, in the Israeli and P.L.O. antagonism, in Poland's union crisis, in El Salvadore, Nicaragua, Afghanistan, Cambodia, and so on in an unending chain of inhumanities, we have never but failed to achieve the reconciliation of our irreconcilable views. I would venture to say that--given the Nietzschean and dehumanizing biases of so many critics--none would remain critics if peace were declared.

[41]Booth, pp. 31-32.   Kenneth Burke levels a brilliant attack against the kind of analogy Booth uses here as a mode of argument.   He calls analogies used as bases for argument "informative anecdotes," and argues that terminologies derived from such anecdotes are transferred to different orders of cases--the matter at hand--and thus are predestined to misrepresentation.   By anecdote, Burke means any situation, experiment, object, condition, complex of events, etc., that the critic uses as the source of his terminology to define a problem in another area.   We have seen in our discussion of De Man's anecdotes of the chair and the marksman how such misrepresentation takes place.   The problem is equally obvious in Booth's use of the cone.   See Kenneth Burke, A Grammar of Motives (Berkeley:   University of California Press, 1969), appendice D. pp. 503-17.

[42]Booth, p. 32.   Booth's phrase here, the "precise mathematical formula for an 'ideal' cone," subverts the entire position his analogy is meant to support.   One could only regard it as a slip--but a revealing one--into former ways of thinking about the literary object.   The "ideal" cone, of course, would transcend all perspectives from the viewpoints of the observers:   this is a monistic attitude, even if Booth argues that the "ideal" could not be achieved in practice--it is still there as the noumenon behind the perspectives of the actual which governs our awareness.

[43]See Michael Murray, Modern Critical Theory:   A Phenomenological Introduction (The Hague:   Martinus Nijhoff, 1975), the chapter "The Critical Present in Prospect and Retrospect," pp. 215-224.   The phenomenological approach to the reader--in the author, work, reader triangle--would have the reader as a fully creative partner in the literary process. The notion that the reader is a passive, external, merely observational awareness, a ground upon which the author works

through the text, is criticized as an aesthetic misconstruction. The phenomenologist turns to Heidegger's view that the reader is the "preserver," to suggest "the special type of creativity native to the experience of poetry." The act of interpretation is the concrete way this act of preservation occurs. In a very thoughtful paragraph, Murray writes, "Man the interpreter constitutes the existential horizon for every possible interpretation, not because he takes a psychological interest in it, or even that special variety called aesthetic interest, but rather on account of man's life-relation to the text . . . . All interpreting partakes in the question of who man is." Within the context of this life-concern, the "pre-understanding" of the text is the phenomenon which orients, indentifies, initiates the basic questions which results in that resolution we call an interpretation (a full or at least the fullest understanding that one can achieve). Thus, "What is understood in interpretive understanding," Murray writes, "is always the text in its meaning" (pp. 221-222). I can accept this view with little qualification--for the conceptual design of a poem, it seems to me, is the necessary initiator of understanding; and the design, when we regard a poem as great or meaningful, is always a shape given to some life-experience. We call works trivial or shallow when this life-experience can readily be seen as predictable, stereotypical, thoughtless.

[44]Murray, p. 222.

# AFTERWORD

During the course of this book, I have myself used and examined the use by others of a variety of analogies--drawn from psychoanalysis, linguistics, logic, physics, technologies of various sorts, mathematics, geometry, biology, etc. It is easy for the critic to feel that his use of analogies constitutes a creative contribution to literary studies; and insofar as the critic's "point" is served by concretization, he has great respect for the power and efficacy for discourse of his creativity--and finds it difficult thereby to understand the difference between his own use of figures for the purposes of discourse and the poetic use of them.

In an article entitled "Mathematical Linguistics and Poetics," one writer argues for the application of information theory to poetics. In this view, poetics--the notion of poetic language--is conceived as "a communication channel" which can be defined by a quantitative measurement of linguistic choices.[1] I think it is only fitting that I should conclude this book with a few words on the difference between "discourse" in general and poetry, which is an issue of increasing significance as far as literary criticism is concerned.

In our present climate of ideological warfare, with the science and technology the various disputants have to concentrate and disseminate their "visions of the world," it becomes increasingly easy to regard the arts as one more means to impress messages upon men. Some critics call for action as a legitimate response to art and regard the poem in particular as a medium of persuasion. The responsibility of the reader, in this view, is to "suspend aesthetic judgment in the interest of right action."[2] But perhaps more common still is the general disrepute into which poetry has fallen; I mean the view that finds the poet and the poem unable to compete any more with the "great" modes of discourse--science, politics, philosophy, and even criticism (which sees itself increasingly as scientific and more interesting than the poetry it once regarded as its province). This view is best stated by one of the many who hold it today--even though his honesty in explicitly avowing it is still rather rare:

> [The] radical truth is this: _The reason no great poetry has been written on these great issues_ [the central political, philosophical and scientific issues of our times] _is that the great minds of our times do not write poetry_. The great minds of our times are directly engaged in the central political, philosophical and scientific issues of the day, and, of critical importance, they are involved in these issues with a mode of discourse which finds the poetic mode insufficient.[3]

If it were not so important, it could be easy to ignore remarks like this. But I'm afraid this view prevails, even among critics, who feel obligated to "cure" their readers of the notion of poetry altogether, having in some instances disabused us of the "concepts" of poet and reader. At one time we insisted that poetry provided us with knowledge and helped us to understand both the natural world and our human experience of it. As science and philosophy began to disabuse us of this faith in our imagination and language, we developed the notion that poetry provided us with mere _forms_ of understanding, that poetry was "purposeless" and "disinterested." We found a new freedom, we thought; finally, as a great poet of our time insisted, we said, "poetry makes nothing happen." Our contemporaries, as Gerald Graff has pointed out, have extended this notion to its final resting place: poetry _ought_ to make nothing happen. Who, then, actively engaging in the great issues of our time, would turn to poetry? The only thing left out of the history of these ideas is, of course, poetry, which has continued to help us, in spite of everything, understand both the world and our experience of it.

But politics, philosophy, science--the realm in which the mind is engaged in problem solving, in which _everything_ that has value has it insofar as it contributes to problem solving--these are essentially techniques for establishing, not human understanding, but human dominance over nature (human nature included). I would also include among these realms contemporary literary criticism, a discipline that has become increasingly enamoured of Nietzsche, who taught us that man's urge to power has only one meaning, one purpose: more power. The will to power is never satisfied and manifests itself in the exercise of that power. Eventually, the one question man cannot help but to ask--What is the purpose of our human effort and industry, of all our spent energy and sacrifice?--is left unanswered, even unasked in a conscious, deliberative way, in a society that conceives of greatness and thus worth in the mind's thrust toward dominance, toward power. The human thirst for a meaning to personal existence that exceeds _nothing_ can never rest in or be satisfied by the exercise of power. The question "Why seek power, what is it all for?" cannot be answered in terms of power itself. The mystery of life remains unexplored even as we unravel it. Is the "mystery of life" a problem to be solved or an experience to be had? I suspect that to speak of it at all as a mystery is to be beyond understanding, because one is using one's problem solving faculties in the act of conception--faculties which are inherently unsuited to comprehend what it sets out to comprehend in the phrase "mystery of life." Shelley believed that the ideas of reason were essentially weapons to be used aggressively in the scientific analysis of nature. Reason, he argued, was a killer because its operation was divisive. Thus the world apprehended by its analytical powers was a dead world--a world without mystery, a world dehumanized.

Our experience of mystery is grounded in the "out there" which is quite indifferent to us, but is nevertheless the source of our being. This may seem paradoxical, for how can the indifferent be the source of value? The answer is never to confuse Being and value. These are distinct. Being exists. But value is an expression of Being. We are too ready in our philosophizing to reverse this ordering of Being and value. To see Being as an expression of value is essentially to find hope in the human condition. It is from this reversal that man becomes the measure of things and the focal point of existence. But the poet's is a vision of human transcience, full of yearning for what was, apprehension for what will be, despair over our human impotence to alter the condition that makes us what we are and the world what it is. The poetic vision apprehends the world as it is before reason and analysis destroy our primitive faith in the observation of our senses, and the nagging pitch of personal death that permeates the poet's awareness is the cry of Being. Nothing we can do will ever silence this cry. Nor should we try. Like the cry of the baby, it irritates us into responsibility. Perhaps, and this intensifies the problem, to think this way is what will in the end condemn us. But the unmediated vision of death is a fundamental experience, the bottom line, which underlies all other ways of feeling. This vision gives value to all thought that departs from it.

It is easier for men to envision cataclysmic, universal death than personal death. Apocryphal terror--fire and brimstone, whirlwind and flood, the war-dragon loosed finally--these images are ultimately satisfying as stimuli of terror, for in them the dread of personal death--the final agony of _my_ body and _my_ mind--are submerged in the imagery of cultural collapse and universal destruction. One can much more readily contemplate universal than personal death--with its menace, its devouring of _me_, hand and foot. All religions have exploited this truth. This truth is the _nothing_ at the heart of everything. Seeing this, how unutterably precious become living things in their fullness. Awareness of this truth is what Lorca meant by "duende" and what underlies and inspires that curiously flip-flopping poem of Thomas', "And Death Shall Have No Dominion." And so our question--What is the purpose of our human effort and industry, of all our spent energy and sacrifice?--comes back doubly hard on us, and power and motivations deriving from the pursuit of it are ultimately felt as mere motions empty of all meaning.

Dispensing with the quest for meaning, as Anglo-American and Existentialist philosophy has attempted this century, leaves man alienated from his ultimate desire. To argue today that man needs a _center_ of meaning in order to validate his existence and provide a moral basis to his life is to be at once old-fashioned and commonplace. Nevertheless, the will to power is both tyrant and slave, a vicious appetite that keeps mankind rushing headlong into an increasingly meaningless and thus insecure future. When Shakespeare wrote in _Troilus_ _and_ _Cressida_ that "everything includes itself in power,/Power into will, will into appetite,/And appetite, a universal wolf,/so doubly seconded with will and power,/Must make perforce a universal prey,/And last eat up himself,"[4] he could not conceive of the terror such an image might hold for us today. How does poetry fit into our world?

To see poetry as a mode of discourse is to see it from the perspective of the will to power; it is essentially to see it as one more exercise of that power, as though the poet were wielding words in an exchange the outcome of which would or could decide an issue. As a "mode of discourse," in this or any other age, poetry is bound to be inefficacious, inferior to the discourses of science and politics, even criticism, for these discourses effect change in the world, place in the hands of their practitioners actual power to heal, sway, alter, kill or learn. Poetry has never done this. In the history of the progress of philosophy and science, poets have always resisted the claim that the human senses cannot apprehend the world as it really is. However often the philosopher has argued that there is no "out there" to form the basis for mimesis in art, the poet responded by imaginatively possessing the world anyway. The result of this possession--the poem--is not discourse. In a manner of speaking, the essence of poetry is to resist the will, to resist its conversion into discourse by those who can see it only as such. This is why to take the contemporary view is already to place oneself beyond the possibility of an answer to our question. To argue that the great minds of our time find the discourse of poetry insufficient to their needs is to see the whole issue through a glass darkly, and to misconceive even what one is talking about. Poetry calls upon us to lay down our will, to assume an attitude, as Heidegger has said, of wise passivity. Why is this so? Why is this not so for "discourse"? And why is poetry so special in this regard among the arts?

Let us take a detour to find our path. Consider what we mean by the word wild. We mean, don't we, that which does not fit into our order of things, that which has not been changed or adjusted to accommodate our ways and manners and abide by our expectations? We might call a new land "wild" until we have established ourselves in it and reduced its infinite possibilities to yield what we need from it. Similarly with an animal. It ceases to be "wild" when we have so altered it that every aspect of its growth and behavior conform to our estimate of the most we can get from it in terms of our needs. But this is really a curious assumption when we think about it. Where men have never been (when there were such places), everything that existed belonged to an order that was natural and adjusted by laws that functioned ruthlessly to keep it stable--even the laws of biological evolution were part of this stability. When man acquired the power to affect this order for his own ends, he became effectively a principle of disorder in this system, and in relation to it mankind and all its works constitute a genuine wildness and everything artificial and cultivated is a wildness whose effects on the natural order will always be unpredictable and at times uncontrollable. It did not take our contemporary awareness of the ecology to teach us this--these thoughts about "wild" are Montaigne's.[5] But in terms of the objectivity of the sciences and of our will to control the world for human purposes, it is impossible to comprehend this curious reversal or flip-flopping of our sense of things. The very faculty of mind that enables one to grasp it is imaginative in the poetic sense and the feeling of assent that accompanies the "seeing" arises from that in us which responds to poetry.

One would not regard music as a discourse, at least not normally. To enjoy music one must give oneself up to it, let it enter oneself, so to speak, without resisting it; and this giving oneself up to the experience is our avenue to enjoyment of music. One does not enter into a dialogue with a melody, one lets its momentary existence take sway over oneself. To try to influence the experience of music by an act of will is to interpose between oneself and the experience a screen from behind which one ceases to hear. This is what happens to poetry when we regard it as a mode of discourse.

It is in the nature of discourse, on the other hand, for one to stand apart from it, to use one's powers if intellection to analyze and respond to it. Discourse requires acts of will in a continuous and unending series of interchanges. In our industrial and scientific culture, discourse is the conduit that synthesizes the thought and effort of the millions of separate people interacting on all levels for the purposes of production. It is, in its nature, blind to everything except what flows through its channels. Passivity in the presence of discourse is a violation of the codes which govern it, and when one is passive on such occasions, his passivity is a rhetorical stance and is paradoxically still a "mode" of discourse. As such, it is unlike the wise passivity that is characterized by giving oneself up. The fundamental character of poetry, as everyone knows, is its articulation of language (which it shares with discourse). Its route, therefore, to our emotions and the value centers of our being is via concepts. In poetry we experience these concepts as we experience melody in music. Thus to give oneself up to poetry is to give oneself up to the experience of Being in the only way humanity can know it, for the beauty of poetry is that it exists only in the experience of it.

In F. H. Bradley's words, "My external sensations are no less private to myself than are my thoughts or my feelings. In either case my experience falls within my own circle, a circle closed on the outside; and with all its elements alike, every sphere is opaque to the others which surrounds it . . . . In brief, regarded as an existence which appears in a soul, the whole world is peculiar and private to that soul."[6] This is a Cartesian vision of human reality. We may rail against it, seek with all our energies to circumvent it, we may even will it to be not so and believe we succeed; but, unless we die and discover through some other agency of awareness that this is an illusion produced by a history of metaphysics, it will always be so for us. For I believe this condition is not dependent upon a way of relating our consciousness to its environment, but is a consequence of being. It is this condition that makes poetry necessary and that makes the poet's revelation in language of his "peculiar and private" soul a human necessity. This condition of subjectivity is the guarantor of the poet's continued relevance to the population he serves; nowhere but in poetry can we find such intimate assurance that the race and the self (ourselves) are one:

then it is not so difficult
to go out, to turn and face
the spaces which gather into one sound . . . the singing
of mortal lives, waves of spent existence
which flow toward, and toward, and on which we flow
and grow drowsy and become fearless again.[7]

(Galway Kinnell)

To treat of poetry as a mode of discourse rather than as a mode of experience is to act upon it and such action constitutes a resistence to what is fundamentally there to be experienced: not "nature" so much as nature humanized, nature as it exists _in_ humanity. When we ask poetry to treat of issues, any issues that we find compelling at any moment in our cultural lives, we are converting it to discourse and abandoning its nature as art.[8] Poetry does not treat; as I find myself stressing on every occasion, to think in these terms is to miss what poetry in fact is and to place oneself beyond understanding. The poet does not observe and treat, he allows to come alive in himself the insistent and pressing realities of composition. It matters, in our scientific age, whether we see ourselves as creators or chance inhabitants of our world. Either we envision Being as entering or becoming our thought or thought as creating Being. The willfulness of the creative/destructive urge in men is a point I need not belabor. It is what we all fear. But there is nothing so humbling as the awareness that what we touch _is_ _not_ _ours_, that Being precedes us and that we are as children at play among our father's things. What the poet _experiences_ is undoubtedly himself, his humanity and his uniqueness, and through what he creates he makes available to us a portion of Being that we could expereince in no other way. What the world _is_ we can know only through ourselves, but knowing the world through ourselves does not lead to the necessity of expressing this knowledge in terms of "myself." Dostoyefsky did not create Ivan/Alyosha by observing people. That this fictional identity is his identity is one of the reasons Nabokov rakes him over the coals. And yet, Nobokov is always Nobokov--a fact he knew but never recognized, that is, "knew." The poet must know these things, as Dostoyefsky undoubtedly did. This is why, in his very superiority to Dostoyefsky, Nobokov falls so far below him. To be unable to value poetry is to be unable to value humanity itself, to be blind to it is to be blind to one's own humanity. Through poetry we experience human being being in the world. Through science we acquire knowledge and power but through poetry we acquire the experience of being of which this knowledge and power is a part, and only a part, and perhaps not even the most important part.

When the geneticist succeeds in controlling our inheritance, how can he appreciate the losses and gains for humanity represented by his manipulations without understanding Human Being as it exists? What are the avenues to such understanding? Should we trust him to judge for us on the basis of his singular sense of being? Or the collective sense of geneticists? Should he turn for an intimate knowledge of what we stand collectively to lose or gain by his power to the sociologist with his graphs and statistics? To whom should he turn for that vivid and intimate experience of nature-in-human-nature by which at least it is possible for him to judge? The ideologue? The Literary Critic? The poet does not give us information as the sociologist does, nor is he concerned with persuasion, with hard thinking of any kind. He is concerned with experience and with the mind as awareness that can be textured with experience. The poet does not compete with the scientist and the politician and the philosopher. Rather, in our culture taken as a whole, he complements them. The poet provides us with the means to a purely personal cultivation, and in doing so he makes available to us a larger humanity, a humanity without which our imaginations would have no place to dwell.

The critic quoted at the outset of this meditation argues that the only truly heroic thing the poet can do in our day is stop writing. What we would stand to lose in a climate which increasingly shares this opinion today is obvious if poets lose their confidence: no less than the collective or racial experience of our species. What would remain to us? The objectivity of the sciences (which in terms of our humanity as a "subject" leads inexorably to Skinner), the intrigues of politics, the manipulations of logic and ordinary human activity guided by a sense of Nothing at the heart of things, a great dissolving nothingness that would ultimately penetrate every joy and every value in human experience. What, then, is poetry? Imagine the child's fourth-of-July toy--the sparkler. It is a long metal shaft, encrusted with hardened powder. It is in fact a solid object. Neglect for the sake of the metaphor the chemical properties latent in the object and awaiting fire as their precipitant. The object is present in all its materiality. Touch it to the flame and fire, in the form of star-like seeds, bursts from it and fills the night with shining. "Imprisoned sparks." Flame sets free the flame. This is a description of the relationship between poetry and language, between creation and being:

> Her face lights up in a golden shining
> and the ground at her feet turns to gold.

Such an image is merely a description of a child, something seen, accurate as far as it goes. But think of "wild" here. Do you see it happening? The darkness of a conditioned way of seeing pushed back revealing what a measurement of light can never tell?

NOTES

[1]Robert Abernathy, "Mathematical Linguistics and Poetics," in Poetics, eds., Roman Jakobson, et. al. (Gravenhage: Mouton & Co'S, 1961), pp. 563-69.

[2]See Ihab Hassan, "Beyond a Theory of Literature," in Issues in Contemporary Literary Criticism, ed. Gregory T. Polletta (Boston: Little, Brown and Company, 1973). Hassan argues that if literature is both cognitive and experimental, "how can new knowledge but prompt new action?" When the work becomes "subject to the total judgment of human passions," the critic cannot criticize timorously; criticism must assume "that final and somewhat frightening responsibility which some critics naturally resist; namely, the willing suspension of aesthetic judgment in the interest of right aciton" (pp. 143-45). In seems to me that if we do come to the poem from the perspective of the "life-relation," then Hassan's argument here drives at the very heart of the literary enterprise, and the task for critics is to find some way to rescue literary effort from the propaganda of our ideological world war. This, however, is another project--all I can hope is that in my conclusion here I do at least point to a way out.

[3]David Perkins, "Response to Frederick Turner," The Missouri Review, Winter (1982), p. 187.

[4]William Shakespeare, Troilus and Cressida, A New Variorum Edition, ed. Harold N. Hillebrand (Philadelphia: J. B. Lippincott Company, 1953), I, iii, 122-30.

[5]See Michel D. Montaigne, "On Cannibals," in _Essays_, trans. J. M. Cohen (Baltimore, Maryland:  Penguin Books, Inc., 1966), pp. 108-09.

[6]This passage, from _Appearance and Reality_, is quoted by T. S. Eliot in the note for lines 412-415 of "The Wasteland": "I have heard the key / Turn in the door once and turn once only / We think of the key, each in his prison / Thinking of the key, each confirms a prison."  The note is presented by Eliot without comment.  It seems to me to require none; in the world of the poem, the lines and the passage by Bradley elegantly evoke the hypermodern sense of alienation that all our philosophizing since has not diminished.  It, too, is at the "bottom line," as I say above, and in part gives value to all thought that departs from it.  But at the same time, language bridges the distance between the worlds, if only we let it; if only do not erect barriers.  See the poem by Matthew Arnold, "To Marguerite"; here, in "the sea of life enisled," as Arnold envisions it, people are eternally separated by "The unplumbed, salt, estranging sea":  "God their severance rules!"  Yet their alienation from each other does not give rise to the "desire" to overcome it until "The nightengales divinely sing; / And lovely notes, from shore to shore, / Across the sounds and channels pour."

[7]From Galway Kinnell, "There Are Things I Tell To No One," in _Mortal Acts, Mortal Words_ (Boston:  Houghton Mifflin Company, 1980), pp. 59-62.

[8]Emerson, in a journal entry, wrote that he could not turn the great issue of the time--slavery--into poetry; the muse would not assist him:  "But the God said, 'Not so; Theme not this for lyric flow . . . .'"  See Aaron Kramer, _The Prophetic Tradition in American Poetry, 1835-1900_ (Rutherford: Fairleigh Dickinson University Press, 1968), p. 333 and note 1, p. 389.

I think Emerson's difficulty is a profound intimation of the difference between discourse and poetry. Emerson could write prose on the subject, could <u>treat</u> the subject argumentatively, but not artistically, not as a poet.